Do Tell!
Stories by Atheists and Agnostics in AA

Edited by Roger C.

AA Agnostica

Copyright

Do Tell!
Stories by Atheists and Agnostics in AA

Library and Archives Canada Cataloguing in Publication

Do tell! : stories by atheists and agnostics in AA / edited by Roger C.

Issued in print and electronic formats.

ISBN 978-0-9940162-3-2 (pbk.).–ISBN 978-0-9940162-4-9 (ebook)

1. Alcoholics–Rehabilitation. 2. Alcoholics Anonymous. 3. Recovering alcoholics–Religious life.

4. Atheists–Mental health. 5. Agnostics–Mental health.

6. Recovering alcoholics' writings.

 I. C., Roger, 1950-, editor II. AA Agnostica, issuing body

HV5278.D665 2015   362.292'86   C2015-902884-1

                                            C2015-902885-X

Published in Canada by AA Agnostica

Cover design by Kyla Elisabeth

Interior layout and eBook version formatted by Chris G.

Table of Contents

Dedication

This book is dedicated to Ernest Kurtz, the author of several books including *Not-God: A History of Alcoholics Anonymous* and *The Spirituality of Imperfection: Storytelling and the Search for Meaning*. He would no doubt have enjoyed the stories in *Do Tell!* As Bill White reports in his Personal Tribute to his mentor and friend: "Ernie was a lover of stories and had a profound belief in the healing power of personal story reconstruction and storytelling".

Foreword

By Marya Hornbacher

Author, *Waiting: A Nonbeliever's Higher Power*

My first impression in the rooms of AA: *This is really weird.*

For starters, I was not drunk – this in itself was a little surreal, and lent the basement room in which I sat an extra-sickly neon cast. Also, I did not entirely know where I was. The people around me looked beatific, glowing through the fog of smoke. There was a suspicious general happiness. Someone offered me a cup of coffee, someone else handed me a banana, the reasons for which remain unclear. I looked around myself in a panic, trying to sort out how I had wandered into what was, I now realized, a church.

A hum of chatter, then a reverent hush – and then a woman bounced up to the podium and shouted gleefully, "Hi! My name is Connie, and I'm a drunk!"

A drunk! I nearly collapsed with relief. I could relate to drunks! Some of my best friends were drunks! I myself was, in fact, a drunk, a fact that hit me in the gut – not for the first time, but perhaps with the greatest force – at that moment. Nothing could have been clearer, and never had it been so clear: I was, as the person next to me whispered reassuringly, "in the right place."

I nodded, my attention now drawn to the large signs that flanked Connie at the podium. They appeared to be lists. I assumed they were the rules for sobering up.

Hopeful, I read them top to bottom, several times.

They made absolutely no sense.

Devastated – if there were rules to this game of sobriety, I wanted to know what they were, and would have done damn near anything I was instructed to do, if it might finally yank me out of the bottle in which I'd been soaking for years – I sat reading the lists, again and again. And all I could really grasp, through my thick-brained haze, were these snippets: Came to believe, God, God, Him, Higher Power, prayer, Power, spiritual awakening.

I left.

That is, I'll admit, a highly selective reading of the Twelve Steps. There are lots of other words, and underneath even the clutter of words are the principles upon which this program rests. Those principles have, in the years since that day in 1989, proven themselves vital, elemental, in my own messy pursuit of an ethical life. But all I got from that first reading of the Steps – and I know I am not alone in this – was exactly what I didn't want. Standing between me and Connie, me and the toxic coffee, me and the drunks in the room where I knew I belonged, was the idea of God.

Do Tell!, this diverse and richly textured collection of recovery stories by non-believers, is a book that would certainly have made a difference in the early days of my stumble toward sobriety and the Twelve Steps. But it is also making a difference in my sobriety today. My evolving understanding of a non-theistic AA has been deepened and changed by this encounter with the stories of people who, like me, "came to believe" that the ethical structure – some call it the spiritual program – that underlies the Twelve Steps could help them rebuild their lives.

The people whose stories are gathered here have come by sobriety honestly, and I suspect some people might say we came by it the hard way. If that's true, the hard way seems to be a perfectly effective way of getting sober. Speaking for myself, taking the easy way kept me frustrated, resentful, and drunk. Trying to find sobriety by swallowing the Steps and the program as they were practiced by other people – rather than as I understood them myself – was as effective as walking around in someone else's ill-fitting skin. This isn't to say I required special steps for my own special sobriety to shore up my fantastically sorry self; it is to say that in order to feel sobriety more deeply, in order to live a sober life at a more than doctrinal level, I needed to grapple with the steps on my own terms.

That is what you will find in these stories: not a recitation of truisms, not a common narrative, not quick or easy answers to life's questions; rather, you will find an engagement with the Steps and the program of AA that is honest, conscious, and hard-won, and perhaps all the more vital for that. These stories tell of people questioning, investigating, identifying, disputing, and challenging not only the traditional interpretations of AA, but also of themselves, always seeking a richer, more intimate understanding of a program that, by hook or by crook, helps keep them on the path of sobriety – a path that isn't laid out for us in advance, but one we need to forge.

But even as I say that, I am quite certain there are people whose sobriety – their valuable, vital, life-saving sobriety – depends on a highly traditional and literal reading of the literature, the principles, and the Steps. The purpose of this book is not to derail, disparage, or disdain people whose understanding of a higher power is theistic or deistic in nature, or whose means of sobriety might be considered religious. The goal is simply to bring other stories to light – those of atheists, agnostics, freethinkers, nonbelievers of all kinds – and these stories help flesh out the idea of what sobriety looks like, how it can be understood and practiced, and what it can ultimately be.

"I am responsible. When anyone, anywhere, reaches out for help, I want the hand of AA always to be there." This, the AA Responsibility Statement, shows our fellowship in its finest light: all-inclusive, open to all comers, unrestricted, and there for the taking should anyone ask. This statement is an invitation to any and all. Whether individual meetings live up to this ideal – whether the conference approved literature resonates with us or seems by turns didactic, uplifting, and absurd – whether the people we meet welcome or resist us – isn't of nearly as much consequence as our own willing- ness to accept the invitation. These stories invite the reader in where some stories have seemed to turn them out.

Do we want sobriety? These stories are testament to the fact that AA can be a critical tool in navigating the waters we traverse as we make our way through our lives. Are we willing to go to any lengths to get sober and live according to ethical principles, or spiritual ones, whichever we prefer? These stories show us that the language of the Steps is not enough to keep us out if we want in. Underneath the black and white of the print on the page, the princi- ples exist – dynamic, subject to interpretation, always in flux, and not listed anywhere in the traditional literature, so far as I can find. The principles are left, whether purposely or not, open-ended and undefined. The principles are not learned and recited by rote; they are encountered, wrestled with, understood, re-understood, and lived out in our own lives.

The stories in this book present not a singular vision of sobriety but a prismatic one; they present not a singular ethic, but a means by which a reader can examine ethics from multiple angles and in multiple lights. There is no attempt to define atheism, agnosticism, or freethinking, no attempt to offer an "alternative" spirituality that might neatly fit into the "God-sized hole" I have heard tell exists in everyone's heart. There are people in this book who were raised atheists, people who left religions, people who avidly sought but did not find a higher power to understand, people who find and practice a method of prayer.

I don't tend to believe any of us are struck sober by mysterious forces, any more than we are struck drunk. We learn sobriety. We learn from people around us at meetings, and from the stories they tell; I learned, and continue to learn, from people both like and unlike me, with stories both similar to and drastically dissimilar from my own. One of my fellow AAs, Lyle, introduces himself each week with enormous cheer, and says that by the grace of God and the blood of Jesus Christ, he is here today. He beams with each introduction that follows; he beams at me, knowing full well we disagree mightily, share not a single demographic feature, not a single article of faith, but have found ourselves in the same church basement at the same time for many years, and have – in those years – seen many other people come and go, some having found a door to sobriety that opens for them, and some not.

I believe this book acts as the open door. The stories gathered here demonstrate that even the most unlikely people have found their way to sobriety through the door to AA. I know that had I found this door while feeling around in the dark for a way out of my alcoholism, I would have heard the principles that underlie the steps more clearly, and sooner. This book – and I venture to say the program – acts as an invitation. See if the principles resonate with you. See if there is an ethical structure here on which you can hang your hat. Find your way to the people in the fellowship with whom you can connect, the people who have the serenity and sobriety you seek. You may find in this program a place in which you can finally settle comfortably into your seat, into your skin, and inhabit the place in the program that is, and always will be, yours.

Welcome.

Reshaping the AA Culture

"Storytelling is the practice and indeed the essential dynamic of AA".

AA historian Ernie Kurtz

Roger C.

Things change.

At least that's been my experience in life. And it's the experience of everyone I have ever chatted with about change and their lives and the world in which we live our lives.

I thought it would all settle down, frankly. That finally when I got old enough change would pretty much cease and I could count on things remaining steady, solid and unchanged.

It didn't turn out that way. In fact, the opposite occurred. My understanding of myself and my relationship with others seems to change almost every day. The great mystery of existence becomes more mysterious by the hour. My ideas about everything evolve. Now that I am sixty-five, I do not understand virtually anything in the same way that I did when I was twenty-five. Or when I was forty-five years old, a young pup then, it seems now.

Because things change.

So what's up with AA?

Founded in 1935 by Bill Wilson and Dr. Bob Smith, the fellowship of Alcoholics Anonymous seems somehow incapable of moving forward, at least in any significant way. It seems stuck in a pre-World War II mindset. And that, quite frankly, is a pretty sad place to be stuck.

Even Bill Wilson recognized the problem.

In a speech given to an AA Conference in 1965, he began by noting that "a million alcoholics have approached AA during the last thirty years". He goes on to estimate that 600,000 had walked away from the rooms of AA, never to come back.

He asks: "How much and how often did we fail them?"

That question is exponentially more revelant today, fifty years after Bill asked it.

And of course the problem is that the fellowship remains shackled to the book *Alcoholics Anonymous*, published in 1939, which in turn is mired in the predominant Christian culture of the United States as it existed in the Thirties and Forties.

Two examples of the out-of-dateness of the Big Book (as it is known, which in itself is revealing): the misogynistic chapter "To Wives" and the condescending and patronizing chapter "We Agnostics". That's already a fifth of the main 164 pages, and it hardly stops there.

The book goes on to share a "suggested" program, the 12 Steps, in which God (or "He" or "Him" or a "Power") is mentioned in six of the Steps. In Chapter 5, "How it Works", we are told that "probably no human power could have relieved our alcoholism" but "God could and would if He were sought".

So, go to an AA meeting, invariably in a church basement, and you will find the 12 Steps brazenly displayed at the front of the room and someone is likely to read "How it Works" (at the beginning of the meeting) and you will be invited to join in the Lord's Prayer (at the end of the meeting). This is called a "traditional" AA meeting.

"How much and how often did we fail them?"

And oddly enough the suggestion that AA might be somewhat "religious" is invariably met with some form of denial. When the General Service Office of AA is asked about various Courts in the United States that have ruled AA to be religious, it refuses to respond because the matter is an "outside issue".

No it's not.

It's an "inside issue" and it needs be dealt with honestly and now.

Which is not to suggest that the Big Book ought to be revised or rewritten. It is what it is. It is a kind of memoir written by middle-class white Christian men seventy years ago. The book shares the experience, strength and hope of these men and of others in AA. And in so doing it does something historical; it lays the foundation for what does work for alcoholics: the very human power of one alcoholic talking to another alcoholic. The support we alcoholics find in the rooms assists us in working towards "a personality change sufficient to bring about recovery from alcoholism" and is the very essence of the fellowship of AA.

And that has everything to do with sharing our stories.

Indeed, many people like the Big Book not for its first 164 pages, but because of the roughly three hundred pages that are devoted to the personal stories of fellow alcoholics in recovery. That section begins with the subtitle: "How Forty-Two Alcoholics Recovered From Their Malady".

We are inspired and we learn from hearing about "what it was like, what happened and what it's like now" from those with the common affliction of alcoholism and addiction. And thus the definition and purpose of AA: "Alcoholics Anonymous is a fellowship of men and women who share their experience, strength and hope with each other that they may solve their common problem and help others to recover from alcoholism".

Our dear friend, the late Ernie Kurtz, said that storytelling is in fact "the practice and indeed the essential dynamic of AA". It is the way we AA members support each other and help guarantee our ongoing recovery.

Thus this book.

The stories in this book are all, of course, by AA members who do not believe that an interventionist deity – a God – had anything at all to do with their recovery from alcoholism. As readers will discover, many struggled mightily "in the rooms" with the idea of God or a Higher Power, wanting to fit in, as Alcoholics Anonymous was their last hope.

Some were nonbelievers from the very beginning. Others, as the life-saving "personality change" in recovery took effect over time, abandoned a belief in God. Most felt unable to be honest at meetings, afraid that what they said would be attacked. If they did "come out of the closet" the consequences were hurtful: other members of AA would often take a condescending Dr. Bob approach ("I feel sorry for you") and warn them that they would pick up again if they did not find God. They often felt dismissed, disparaged and rejected in the rooms of traditional AA.

But they stayed, as so many do not. And survived. And are here today to share their stories.

As readers make their way through the book, it will also be noted that a number of writers talk about doing their own version of the 12 Steps.

This too is not without controversy in AA.

So let's start off by asserting that nobody wants to change the original and official Steps of AA, published in *Alcoholics Anonymous* in 1939. No vote needed, understand?

However, it is perfectly normal – indeed inevitable – that the Steps will be intepreted and personal versions created. If God is meant to be "as we understood Him" then surely it goes without saying that we shall do the Steps "as we understand them". The author of the Steps understood that but, somehow, the point is missed in traditional AA: "We must remember that AA's Steps are suggestions only. A belief in them as they stand is not at all a requirement for membership among us. This liberty has made AA available to thousands who never would have tried at all, had we insisted on the Twelve Steps just as written". (Bill Wilson, *Alcoholics Anonymous Comes of Age*, p. 81)

And so from time to time, our writers will share their own version of the Steps. Interestingly, creating one's personal version of the Steps can often be liberating. Neil F. in Chapter 19, "My Journey", writes: "Due to my fear of not fitting in, of not being accepted in AA, I was not open about my atheism when speaking in AA until after I wrote an article 'Personalizing the Twelve Steps' that was published on AA Agnostica in January of 2013. This article was really my full disclosure of my atheism, my becoming totally honest".

Dear readers, the issue of being "totally honest" is at the very heart of this book.

There are a total of thirty stories in *Do Tell!* None of them have been sanitized nor are they cliché-ish in the way that many AA stories appear to be in either the AA Grapevine or in "Conference approved" literature.

No, these are personal and honest stories. All unique, all different. The stories in the book alternate between those by women and those by men and so we discover early on – if we did not appreciate this already – that the factors involved in addiction and recovery are often quite different in the lives of men and women.

Moreover, the style and tone of each author is different. As a consequence, readers will like some stories more than others. That's okay. Early on in AA we learn to take what we need and leave the rest. Nevertheless there is without doubt something in each one of these stories that will resonate with those of us who have lived part of our lives in the struggle for recovery.

The authors come from all parts of North America and the United Kingdom. The length of sobriety of each of them varies considerably, much like at a regular AA meeting, with the average being roughly twenty-one years. Five of the writers have more than forty years of continuous sobriety.

So why this book? Why now? And why is it published by AA Agnostica?

The answer to these questions comes in two words, "refusal" and "failure".

Over the past 70 years the AA Grapevine has published approximately forty stories by agnostics and atheists in AA. That's just a bit better than one every two years. A formal request was made to the Grapevine to publish this collection of stories – spanning the years from 1962 to 2015 – in a book. They had published similar books in the past such as, for example, *Sober & Out*, a collection of stories by gays, lesbians and the transgendered in AA.

The AA Grapevine Board of Directors met on January 29, 2015, and, after a "lengthy discussion", refused the request. No reason was provided.

That's the "refusal" part. Now the "failure".

The General Service Conference is the purported "group conscience" of the AA Fellowship. It meets annually and is composed of approximately 20 directors and staff at AA and the Grapevine, 21 trustees and 93 delegates representing various areas across North America. The Conference, via its Literature Committee, decides on the contents of pamphlets and books which will be published by Alcoholics Anonymous, otherwise known as "Conference approved" literature.

Let's put aside the appalling and inevitable element of censorship in the process just described, at least for now, and point out that over the past forty years, numerous requests have been made to the Conference to publish literature by and about agnostics and atheists in AA. The requests began in 1976 when a subcommittee of the trustees Literature Committee wrote that literature of this kind "is needed to assure non-believers that they are not merely deviants, but full, participating members in the AA Fellowship without qualification".

The requests have been ignored or explicitly denied. Given the rather obvious and growing need for such literature this can only be described as a repeat "failure" on the part of the General Service Conference.

Thus, again, this book.

And perhaps everything is exactly as it should be, in the end.

AA as an organization is a non-organization or an inverted triangle with authority at the grassroots, at the membership and group level.

And at that level there is an explosion of agnostic, atheist and free-thinker AA groups that have been formed over the past few years. You can find these now in the United States, Canada, the United Kingdom, Australia, France and Japan, with more bursting forth every day.

Moreover, in 2014, the first We Agnostics, Atheists and Free Thinkers (WAAFT) international convention was held in Santa Monica, California with three hundred people from around the world in attendance. Another convention is in the works for 2016 in Austin, Texas.

Five years ago there was no literature at all for atheists and agnostics in AA.

Now there is a plethora of good literature: *Waiting: A Nonbeliever's Higher Power* by Marya Hornbacher (2011); *An Atheist's Unofficial Guide to AA* by Vince H. (2011); *A Freethinker in Alcoholics Anonymous* by John Lauritsen (2014); *Common Sense Recovery: An Atheist's Guide to Alcoholics Anonymous* by Adam N. (2015); *Beyond Belief: Agnostic Musings for 12 Step Life* by Joe C. (2014);

and, *The Little Book: A Collection of Alternative 12 Steps* by Roger C. (2014).

To name but a few!

And now this book, the one in your hands that you are reading now, *Do Tell! Stories by Atheists and Agnostics in AA*.

And one of the points of the book, dear readers, is this: We are not going anywhere. Atheists and agnostics are members of AA. Because we say so. As Nell Z. puts it in Chapter 1, "Carrying the Message to the Nonbeliever": "All other factors aside, whenever there is a desire to stop drinking, the answer to the question, 'Can AA work for me?' is a resounding YES. I am an agnostic and a proud member of Alcoholics Anonymous".

For we agnostics to feel at home in the rooms of AA we must inevitably be a part of reshaping the AA culture. We need to be a part of bringing our fellowship into the twenty-first century and helping it let go of its increasingly quaint religious origins.

Alcoholics Anonymous can indeed widen its gateway and be inclusive of all, including atheists and agnostics.

And for that we are responsible.

Things change.

1. Carrying the Message to the Nonbeliever

Nell Z.

"The first time I came into an AA meeting, I felt right at home."

I have heard this shared at group level time and time again. I can imagine the sensation of peace and relief that this discovery of belonging must bring for the alcoholic who immediately feels "at home". Unfortunately, this was not my experience.

My name is Nell, I am an alcoholic, and the first time I came into an AA meeting I felt like I had to squeeze past God to get through the door.

Let me back up, so as not to create the assumption that AA was the initial cause of this discomfort. I have been an agnostic since childhood, so I've felt out of place as long as I can remember, even when among others who shared my abilities and interests. My parents raised me to believe in God, and everyone in the world around me seemed to share in this view, so I did what we alcoholics do best: I pretended from very early on. I was worried that if I didn't pretend, I wouldn't fit in, and I wanted so desperately to belong. I pretended to believe in God until my parents checked me into a Christian-based residential treatment center. I left the first day, and after that, the cat was out of the bag.

I spent the next decade under the influence, in and out of meetings on court cards, telling people that AA was never going to work for me because of "the God thing". The truth is, I just wasn't ready to stop drinking. Then one day, all of a sudden, I was. I got the gift of desperation. I realized that I was done drinking, but I had no idea how to stay sober. I had no answers. All I knew was that there were millions of people in AA who had done it before me. I was willing to do anything it took, and if it meant I could avoid a tragic alcoholic death, then I would figure out some way to believe in God if that was what I had to do to stay sober.

No successes, not even small ones, have arisen from attempting to turn myself into a believer. No matter how I have tried to shape and redefine God into a concept that satisfies me enough so that I can believe, my efforts are always in vain. It is like trying to cram a square peg into a round hole; it will never fit. I want to believe, I really do. I just can't. A fellow AA nonbeliever once suggested to me that maybe we are missing the "God" part of our brains. This seems like an entirely likely explanation, since I become frustrated by trying to believe, much like a patient with aphasia becomes frustrated when trying to speak. He won't be able to, no matter how hard he tries, because the structure is simply not intact. "Higher Power" was of no help to me either. There are lots of powers greater than me. To choose one seemed negligent of the rest, and to call it "mine" seemed unnecessarily possessive.

Step One was easy enough. I qualify as an alcoholic; of this I am absolutely sure. Fortunately, during the last of my many incarcerations, I had an experience that removed my obsession to drink. It was a "moment of clarity", a cognitive shift, or a psychic change, if you prefer. As an agnostic, I did not try to explain this in terms of either God removing my obsession or a chemical change in my brain. I was just grateful for the experience. The important thing for me to remember is that if I want to continue living, I have to acknowledge the fact that I am one of those people who cannot drink no matter what.

Step Two proved to be a bigger challenge. My sponsor instructed me to construct a God of my own understanding, and I called her each night in tears, unsatisfied with my designs. They were ridiculous, flawed, and implausible. My knowledge of existence is so limited that I felt it much safer to avoid speculation entirely. One thing's for sure though: If I create God, I'm bound to get it wrong. I've been making a mess of things my whole life. And what was the point of this silly exercise, anyway? I know I'm not in charge. I know there is very little in this world that I have any say in. I am just a grain of sand on the beach, an insignificant speck of dust in an infinite universe.

Then she said a brilliant thing to me, words that I've since repeated to many newcomers. "Honey", she said, "if trying to have a higher power is making your recovery worse, then stop".

So I did.

Just as none of us share the exact same environmental upbringing or biological hardwiring, everyone's spiritual journey is different. In AA, the journeys that are often spotlighted are those of the atheists and agnostics who come to believe. The long-term atheists and agnostics often remain unidentified, hiding in the shadows, scared to express their take on spirituality. What about those who come in as nonbelievers and retain their skepticism? What about those who come in unsure, only to discover they are atheists? Beliefs are fluid and forever changing, sometimes quickly, sometimes slowly. But one thing is certain: they do not progress in one direction along a continuum. Not all of us "come to believe".

The sensation of being uncomfortable in my own skin and in AA continued throughout my early recovery. When I spoke my truth at meetings, I was often chastised, sometimes even at the group level through cross-talk. I heard a seasoned old-timer brag at several meetings that he refuses to sponsor men who don't believe in God. One woman told me that if I didn't come to believe, I would surely relapse. I tried not to take offense to this; relapse is still a "yet" for me, and the future of everyone's sobriety is uncertain anyway. Still, I felt out of place, so I sought out other nonbelievers.

One day, I discovered a group of like-minded individuals who also suffered from alcoholism and held an AA meeting in a non-prayer format. There, I finally found comfort and a sense of belonging. For the first time, I was home, and it was such a relief to be among people who shared similar views. Many of them had multiple decades of sobriety, and they showed me how to stay sober in ways that made sense to me.

Because of the integral role that this meeting format played in my early recovery, I felt compelled, with the help of other atheists and agnostics, to start a meeting of the same format on the Monterey Peninsula, where such a meeting did not yet exist. We called it "Freethinkers", which is the name adopted by various other non-prayer AA groups throughout the nation.

Getting our meeting listed on the schedule through our local central office was no easy task, however. It was a year-long battle of votes and re-votes, principles and personalities clashing. We were treated as a separatist movement, which reaffirmed the growing conviction I had that atheists and agnostics in AA are often devalued, marginalized, and suppressed. This was most aptly illus-trated by a question asked of me by a member of the steering committee: "Why does your group even want to be on the schedule?" He seemed perplexed, genuinely baffled by something that struck me as so simple and obvious. We want to be on the schedule because we are alcoholics, we are members of AA, and we want to be treated equally among AA groups. Most importantly, though, we want to carry the message.

The spiritual principles of AA, such as honesty, open-mindedness, willingness and brotherly love, can be practiced by anyone, God-believer or not. Some say that AA works for the people who want it. Others say that AA works for the people who need it. I say AA works for the people who DO it. For me, AA is a program of self-improvement. When it comes to my humanity, my sobriety and my recovery, I prefer solutions that are tangible, practical, and achievable to those that are magical, abstract and elusive.

I equate my spirituality to my humanistic journey toward genuine human connection, service, love, and kindness, and the direct practice of the principles advocated by AA. For me, spirituality has nothing to do with beliefs. It has only to do with action. I achieve spiritual fitness through the things that I do (and avoid doing) with the goal of being the best possible version of myself that I can be in any given moment.

In my eyes, AA is a wonderful program with idealistic traditions that are often warped in their execution by imperfect human beings.

A conclusion that I have reached, based on my continued stay in AA and the endless variety I observe in personalities around me at meetings, is this: The program of Alcoholics Anonymous can work for anyone, anywhere, and under any circumstances. It doesn't matter what you've done or haven't done. It doesn't matter who you are or what you believe. It doesn't matter what sort of trials and tribulations you have to walk through in sobriety. Take what you want and leave the rest; the program works if you work it.

In trying to find a higher power, I was trying to fix something that isn't broken. I am who I am, and in a program geared toward rigorous honesty as a spiritual ideal, "fake it til you make it", or otherwise pretend to believe in something that I don't, is counter-productive to my recovery. I am happy, joyous, and free when I practice spiritual principles. This formula applies to everyone, believers and skeptics alike. There is no "maybe" with respect to AA being a spiritual program. It absolutely is, by my definition, and is open to everybody, with the only requirement for membership being a desire to stop drinking. Everything else, from the steps to the clichés and clever quips, are pure suggestion. The popular myth, that AA is a religious cult or demands a belief in a higher power, needs to be dispelled, and I believe that the agnostic meetings help accomplish this.

Before I discovered the "Freethinkers" meeting, I was straddling the threshold, wondering if it was really true that I could use AA to stay sober without having to believe in God. I shudder to think of how many relapses may have followed had I not found that meeting on the local schedule and decided to attend. I had to first feel comfortable going to meetings before I could enjoy going to meetings. It took this initial experience, this softening of the blow in the form of a non-prayer meeting, to squeeze through the door past everyone else's God and anchor myself into the seat, exactly where I belonged.

I enjoy going to meetings of all sorts now… prayer or non-prayer, church or Alano club. The forum and the format no longer intimidate me; I finally found somewhere that I fit in. As a naïve newcomer, I honestly thought my rejection of God put me in a very small minority. In reality, this couldn't be further from the truth.

All other factors aside, whenever there is a desire to stop drinking, the answer to the question, "Can AA work for me?" is a resounding YES. I am an agnostic and a proud member of Alcoholics Anonymous. And, until the day arises when I decide to lift a drink to my lips and destroy my life for a second time, I'm not going anywhere.

2. A Magnificent Game Changer

Doris A.

Like many, childhood was a fertile ground for becoming an alcoholic.

My mother had very serious problems with alcohol, binge drinking though her pregnancies and a good part of my childhood. While there were interesting and wonderful things about both of my parents, and childhood memories that still make me smile, there were serious problems in our home. Whether drunk or sober my mother, in the blink of an eye, became erratic and volatile, even violent at times. My dad was not as mercurial, but he was emotionally stunted; shame was his primary tool for parenting.

My mom got sober when I was 10; it was a gift to all of us, yet it did not bring peace and happiness to the family. Sobriety did not resolve my mother's mental illness nor did it help her troubled marriage. Her enthusiasm for AA and her gift for "program talk" were often coupled with nutty behavior. It was confusing to say the least. By the time I left home I felt like I had gotten off the Titanic with a life raft full of holes.

The first time I drank I was twelve years old; I drank myself into a blackout. Surprisingly my drinking during high school was not all that dramatic. But once I left home to attend college I was off to races. I drank hard and I drank often. I felt liberated by alcohol; it was a psychic lubricant that provided a social ease I do not come by naturally.

But deep in a recess of my brain I knew I had a problem. My drinking had an edge and sloppiness to it, and my blackouts were frequent. I remember one morning in my third year of college waking up with a very severe hang-over. I had to be at school within an hour, so without missing a beat I poured a couple shots of vodka into my soda which I took on the bus to class. This was my "Houston we have a problem" moment; a thought I quickly tucked away in a mental file labeled "to be dealt with later".

After graduation I had no idea what to do next. That year my parents had divorced. My father decided to move to another part of the country, with my younger sister in tow. My mom then literally packed everything she owned in her car, drove around the country aimlessly and then decided to live in a town not far from my father. I was accepted into graduate school but instead followed my family. It was a bit surreal.

Within a short time my mother was diagnosed with late stage cancer. I set aside thoughts of grad school or a professional job and instead worked in a tavern, drank with the bar flies and watched my mother die a horribly painful death. My drinking was rough that year, I was lost and confused, and then I felt orphaned.

Six months after my mother died I hit the reboot switch and moved to the coast. I settled in one of the nicest cities in the country and immediately it felt like home. I knew I could do better than working in a bar, and I wanted to slow down my drinking. Not ready to give it up, but I figured I could change the trajectory.

During the next several years I embedded myself in a social scene that was not about alcohol, hoping that through osmosis I would become a non-problem drinker. I found bright, interesting friends who preferred hiking or talking about books and politics over getting loaded. I met the man I would marry and spend 21 years with, and whom I loved dearly. I entered graduate school and started a career.

During this period I used smoke and mirrors to hide my problem. I was the one who went back to the kitchen for "more ice" and then poured a few more ounces of alcohol in my drink. I had half a bottle of wine before going out with people who rarely had more than a drink or two with dinner. I stopped in a bar for a drink on my way home from work or school. Garden variety alcoholic behavior.

My husband had no experience with alcoholics and was naive about all the tell-tale signs. But after we were married a year and bought our own home things changed. Within a matter of months I started drinking heavily, daily, and secretly. This went on for a year until one day I woke up, went to the phone book and called a drug and alcohol hotline. I was referred to a counselor who told me I needed to go into outpatient treatment and I needed to tell my husband. What followed were many years of trying to stay sober, not trying to stay sober, and everything in between. I never once denied being an alcoholic, but for reasons I don't fully understand I could not totally surrender.

Shortly after the first call for help I started attending AA. A part of me, the part of me that is resilient and intuitive, knew from the beginning that I had no chance of success without the fellowship. But AA was full of land mines. The biggest problem at first was having to sit in a room hearing all the clichés and AA talk that I heard as a kid from my nutty mother. There was almost a PSTD quality to seeing all those "easy does it signs" on the wall and hearing people recite the Serenity Prayer.

Layered on this was the god talk in AA. By the time I entered the program I was an agnostic that wasn't ready to be an atheist. The concept of spirituality seemed benign enough. But the idea of a god that would take an interest in relieving me of alcoholism while ignoring the unimaginable suffering of others seemed childish, and just plain wrong. I so badly needed other language to help me develop some type of road map, but it was hard to find. Being a non-believer in AA is not easy. However, I actually have more resentment toward treatment professionals who told me that if I didn't get god and do the 12 steps as prescribed I would die. I am sure there are many reasons sobriety was so elusive, but being an atheist was not one of them.

Over the years I collected sober time, a few years here a few years there. Often it was a string of months. Some of the drinking periods were well hidden until there was some dramatic incident and the game was over for a while. I also added prescription drugs to the mix – painkillers and sedatives.

Although my sense of self became pretty fractured and compart-mentalized, I still had the side of me that approximated normal. I was well-regarded professionally, I had many interests, and I had a stable seeming marriage as well as many personal relationships that mattered dearly to me. But my addiction had me by the throat and I acted in ways that still make me cringe to think about. I did crazy things in order to drink, was impaired at work, lied with the skill of a sociopath, acted out in a million other ways, and deeply hurt others.

By the time I hit my late 40s alcohol was taking a toll on all aspects of my life. Approximating normal was no longer easy. I was losing any margin of error. I was severely depressed and anxious and had no vision of being able to stop for good.

Around age 50 I was diagnosed with early stage cancer. Since watching my mother die from cancer in her fifties I had been scared of this for decades, but I was lucky that it was found in the nick of time. I elected to have chemotherapy and was provided with the best medical care imaginable. One would think that this would be the most obvious time to finally get sober. But it wasn't. I drank a few times during the year of treatment. If chemotherapy hadn't kicked my ass so hard I am sure I would have drank more.

About a month after being given a clean bill of health, I had one of those "fuck it" moments. Instead of going to work one morning I took a sedative and bought a bottle. I don't remember much that day but later learned I had driven my car into the edge of a golf course, ran over a sprinkler system and then drove home.

For my husband this was the final straw. He asked me to leave the house or go to a 90 day treatment program. I didn't know if I could survive another stay in treatment and reached out to family. My brother kindly offered to have me live with him and his wife to get myself sorted out. I packed a few bags and moved back across the country.

The year that followed was profoundly painful. I was demoralized beyond words, I was still a mess from chemotherapy and my heart was deeply broken. I did immerse myself in AA, got a sponsor, found a therapist and tried to cobble together a few friends. I drank a few times too. About a year after moving I went back to visit my husband to sort out our marriage. When I came back I shut myself in my room with large amounts of alcohol and drank for many days.

This was my bottom, but a divine intervention is not what saved me. What did were two people from the fellowship who showed up to help me get the professional care I needed. I had a circle of friends from AA who didn't flinch. I had a compassionate and skilled therapist who was there with open arms to help. And I had some wee voice in my head that wanted to live.

It took a while for my life not to hurt so much. My husband asked for a divorce and then later remarried. It has taken a very long time to grieve all the losses that have resulted from my drinking. So much time was lost.

But today I can easily say that the gift of having real sobriety is broad and deep, and very tangible. I have gained emotional maturity and am sturdier inside. Life makes sense to me now and most days I feel engaged and content. When I am feeling or acting like a head case I know the things to do to get me back on track. I have better skills at managing my emotions and having honest relationship with others. I am still me, warts and all, but the dark passenger that lives inside of me has gotten very small. Self-destructive urges no longer have the keys to the car.

My alcoholism runs deep, and it is lethal. I am certain that I will always need to be an active member of AA. Having finally tapped into a small but real segment of AA that believes sobriety is possible without god has been a magnificent game changer. I am now more than ever inspired to do service work in the program, so that others like me can find a comfortable seat in the rooms of AA.

I have heard people say that they are grateful for being an alcoholic. I am not one of them. Next time around I would like to be more normal and also to be better at math. But alcohol and drug addiction were in the cards dealt to me. So like every other human being on the planet, all I can do is strive to make the most of my life, to be a half decent person and to love others. I am grateful for having a fellowship – my tribe – that offers me a solution, as we say, one day at a time.

3. I Lost My Faith and Happily So

John S.

It's hard to believe, but it was twenty-six years ago when I attended my first AA meeting, and fortunately I've been sober ever since. The circumstances that brought me to AA are far from unique. I was a young man who's drinking quickly spun out of control. It wasn't an overnight thing, like one day I could drink normally and the next day I was a hopeless drunk, but looking back I can see there were warning signs.

I remember my first drink as if it were yesterday. In fact, it's one of my clearest childhood memories. It was Thanksgiving dinner and my mother thought it would be nice to teach me to drink like a gentleman. She poured a glass of wine, which I instantly loved. It was good in every respect, but more importantly it made me feel different, and though I didn't know it at the time, that was one of my deepest needs, to change the way I felt. I downed the stuff and asked for more. My mother, amused, told me to sip it like a gentleman, but I couldn't do it. I could never do it.

I drank through High School to overcome my social unease yet it drove me deeper into isolation. I drank in college for fun and acceptance, but even my wild fraternity brothers realized that my drinking was somehow different. At 19, I pondered going to AA, but decided I was too young to be an alcoholic. Today, I know better, and I realize that normal drinkers don't sit around wondering if they should go to AA. If you have reached that point, in my opinion, for what it's worth, you may be an alcoholic.

As my drinking got worse, I became increasingly depressed and desperate. I didn't know anything about religion, but it was the 1980s and televangelism and the Moral Majority were in their heyday. Depressed and hopeless, I watched Pat Robertson on television make incredible claims of what God would do. I read the Bible cover to cover, took a class on the New Testament as litera-ture, and I prayed daily to Jesus for help.

I recall one particular episode of the 700 Club when Pat claimed that if I only had the faith of a mustard seed, that God would answer my prayers. In other episodes, God would cast out demons, cure disease, make people happy, but only if they really believed he would. My understanding was that he, God, would basically do as I asked, as long as I sincerely believed he would.

It was during this period when my mother committed suicide by drug overdose. I was with her, watching her run away from this life. I did my best to believe that God would answer my prayers while the paramedics frantically worked to bring her back. It was useless. I was simply incapable of making a connection with the creator of the universe, so I abandoned the God experiment and for the next five years, I was drunk much of the time. I accumulated three DUIs, and my employer, who previously offered me several avenues of help, was ultimately left with no choice but to fire me.

Alone with my fear and desperation, I was driven to my first AA meeting. It was here where I heard for the first time, "My name is so and so and I'm an alcoholic". That stunned me when I heard it, but as people told their stories, I could see that they shared with me and I with them, the terrifying experience of losing ourselves to alcohol, losing control of our own lives.

At the end of the meeting they motioned me to the center of the room where they formed a circle, held hands and prayed, "Our father who art in heaven, hallowed be thy name…" It was the first time I ever experienced holding hands and praying out loud with other people, and I remember feeling embarrassed like I wouldn't want to be seen doing this. It really made me uncomfortable, but I was desperate and when they told me to "keep coming back", I did. In no time I was praying the "Our Father" as if I were Billy Graham himself.

During the first year or two of sobriety, life was difficult but gradually getting better. I was meeting new friends from all walks of life and making amazing discoveries about myself. There seemed to be more God talk in those days than what I hear now, but it was made palatable with assurances that I could choose my own conception of a higher power. I didn't have to believe in any religion or anyone else's conception of God.

Yet, in meetings people would stress the importance of "the drill", which is to start your day on your knees and ask God for a day of sobriety, go to a meeting, call your sponsor, and at night return to your knees and thank God for the day of sobriety. Often in meetings people would claim they did this drill every day, and that they never knew of a single case of anyone getting drunk, who began the day on their knees in prayer. I would sometimes wonder to myself if this were really true.

I studied our book *Alcoholics Anonymous* (also known as the Big Book) with my sponsor. I read passages and chapters repeatedly, many to the point of memorization and gradually progressed through the steps. I went on many "twelve step calls" to carry the message of sobriety to the suffering alcoholic. I visited detox centers, hospitals, jails, prisons, and even people's homes. I saw it all. I experienced alcoholism up close in all its ugliness. I was as the Big Book puts it, "on the firing line".

Shortly after I reached ten years of sobriety my father unexpectedly died. His death stunned me. He seemed bigger than life, career military, Vietnam combat veteran, fluent in German, and well versed in Shakespeare. Yet it only took three days for some microscopic virus to ultimately bring him down. I saw the fear of death in his eyes, followed by a desperate fight to live, and finally acceptance of his fate. We told one another, "I love you", and that was it. He was gone.

After he died, I realized there was much that I had not accomplished and time was slipping away. I was thirty-six years old, and still had not graduated from college, never married, never owned a home, and never made much money. I soon went into a mad rush to change all of that. I enrolled in college, started dating, and I found myself spending less time in the AA halls than I had in the past. Within two years, I finished my college degree, bought a home, and had a steady relationship. In another couple of years, I bought my first new car, had a nice job with my own office, and proposed to my wife on the same day that I that earned my MBA degree.

I entered a new phase of life where AA was no longer the center of my existence. It was only one part of who I was, and I began to question everything. My wife who I married in 2006 is an atheist and the first atheist that I ever knew very well. She's not at all like the atheists I heard described by an early sponsor. He would often say that atheists were some of the unhappiest people he ever knew.

Well my wife is one of the happiest people that I've ever known. She has a good sense of humor, she loves people, animals, and good books, and she enjoys life to the fullest. Though others around her seem to go through much drama, myself included, she remains amazingly even keeled. And she's an atheist!

Perhaps influenced by my wife's example, I read the book *God is Not Great*, by Christopher Hitchens. I was quite secretive about reading it, and I certainly wouldn't dream of talking about it with my AA friends. However, that book changed the way I thought about religion, spirituality and AA. I next read Richard Dawkin's *The God Delusion*, and I became interested in evolution and the workings of the universe. I found that reality as explained by science was far more beautiful than the best story concocted by any religion.

I had gone past the point of no return and I didn't want anything to do with spirituality or God. But how was I to work the AA program? Would I ever come clean with my AA friends? Would they still like me? Although AA was no longer the center of my life, it was the cornerstone, it was the bedrock upon which I had built a new life, and I no longer believed or wanted to believe much of what I had been talking about, thinking about, and doing for so many years.

There's a chapter in the Big Book titled "We Agnostics" where an effort is made to convince agnostics and atheists that belief in a higher power is practical, and that recovery from alcoholism is possible only through a spiritual experience. I used to swallow this chapter hook, line and sinker, but I now see it as totally absurd, and it's completely against my world view.

When I learned that there are AA groups consisting primarily of atheists, agnostics and freethinkers, I found it strange that they would name their groups after this chapter, but it makes sense to me now. I see it as the atheist alcoholic's declaration of independence, announcing to the AA community that this chapter leaves us unconvinced. We are still agnostic and still sober.

I started exploring the Internet for more information and my search led me to some people who formed an online community for atheists in AA. I would later meet one of these people, R.J., in Omaha and we had a great time talking about atheism, AA, the Big Book, the future of AA, you name it. I became energized and excited about the program and I still look forward to my weekly meetings with R.J.

Today, I find AA more meaningful when I am free to think about the steps without feeling compelled to conform to the party line. Recovery is real when removing the supernatural aspect. I still find some good in the Big Book and though the language is more than dated, I do think it speaks to the experience of alcoholics, and I believe the AA program works. It's just that I now find the religious language divisive and unnecessary.

Inspired by R.J. and sites such as AA Agnostica, I helped to start a We Agnostics AA meeting in Kansas City with Jim C., the only other atheist I knew in Kansas City AA. Our group is off to a nice start. We have a comfortable meeting place and a core group of people committed to its success. I've seen people come to our group who were avoiding AA because of the religious nature of other meetings, or who left years ago but returned after learning about our meeting. We support one another and we're genuinely excited about helping others.

Our experience reminds me of a passage from the Big Book taken from the chapter "A Vision for You" that describes AA as a place where "…you will find release from care, boredom and worry. Your imagination will be fired. Life will mean something at last. The most satisfactory years of your existence lie ahead. Thus we find the fellowship, and so will you".

Thanks to other agnostics, atheists and freethinkers in AA, this is how I feel about the program today.

4. Returning to My Spiritual Roots in Sobriety

Julie B.

I'm an urban Aboriginal woman who was raised by a single mother of European descent.

Although I did beadwork and occasionally went to powwows, I didn't subscribe to – and was never really exposed to – any traditional Anishinaabe cultural practices or spiritual beliefs. Now that I'm sober, I consider myself to be a spiritual person, and an agnostic.

The only spiritual connection I felt when I was drinking was worshipping my next bottle of wine. Before getting sober, I drank heavily for over 20 years, and drank daily for the last 10. I was high-functioning for someone with extremely low expectations. For a long time, I knew that I was an alcoholic, but I didn't care.

I grew up without religion in my home, and although I was very curious to find a religion that I could adopt, none ever felt right to me. In my quest to belong, I went to several different church services, read the bible, went to Sunday school and joined a church group. I read books on Taoism and Buddhism. I really wanted to believe in something greater than myself, and belong to a community that shared those beliefs, but I couldn't do it while being honest with myself. So I eventually stopped searching for religion.

There are alcoholics on both sides of my family, and I grew up in a house where drinking, drug use and abuse were part of the family dynamic. I suppose I'd been searching for religion or something similar, in order to find an escape from the traumatic events I faced at home on a daily basis. The escape I found was alcohol.

From what I've been told, I started drinking when I was a baby. I was told that my dad put beer in my bottle so that I would go to sleep. I remember my interest in alcohol began in my early teens. When I drank, I felt an instant relief and escape from my home life. When I went drinking with my friends, I felt like I finally belonged to something. I was kicked out of the house when I was 16, and to support myself, I worked as a waitress. I eventually became a full-time bartender, and worked in bars and restaurants for over 20 years. Looking back, I built my life around being able to drink. I could drink at work, I didn't have to wake up early in the morning, and I never learned to drive a car. I had a job with low expectations, and I spent my free time drinking.

I remember being very aware that I was at risk to become an alcoholic. I knew that my family history of addiction and trauma put me at a high risk for alcoholism, and that I should be careful. None of the statistics taught me how to avoid being an alcoholic. I knew the risks, but that didn't stop me from consuming alcohol at an ever-increasing rate. It wasn't until I wanted something more for my life that I realized I was an alcoholic. It was probably another five years after that realization that I decided to do something about it.

When I finally sought treatment, I was drinking almost constantly from the time I woke up, to the time I passed out at night. I had tried to stop repeatedly, but I couldn't, and that scared the hell out of me.

I started treatment on a part-time, outpatient basis, and began attending agnostic AA meetings. After three years of attending meetings, I can honestly say that I feel like I finally found somewhere that I belong. I'm very grateful that these meetings exist, because at the time I was convinced that AA was a religious cult, which had always been my excuse for not seeking help in the past. The treatment centre I went to used a harm reduction model, which I initially hoped would work for me. I was overwhelmed by the idea that I could never drink again for the rest of my life. I was afraid that the people in AA were going to judge my choice, but I was offered support as I attempted to maintain moderate drinking. So, with the aid of medication, individual counselling and group therapy sessions, I worked diligently to adhere to safe drinking guidelines. Looking back, the amount of time, money and effort I put into trying to drink non-alcoholically was ridiculous, but now I know that harm reduction doesn't work for me. I found this out the hard way on a long weekend in July of 2011, when I really hit bottom.

Canada Day weekend of 2011, most of my friends were out of town, including my boyfriend and roommate. I had to work all weekend, but for some reason I decided that I could abandon my controlled drinking plan for the weekend and no one would know. After the first day home alone with several bottles of wine, I knew I was in trouble. The next day I could barely make it to work, and when I got there, they sent me home. By the final day of the long weekend, I was calling everyone I knew for help, because I couldn't stop drinking. My sister finally came to my rescue. She called my work and told them I wouldn't be coming in, instructed me to take a shower and took me out to dinner. When she left my apartment with all of my liquor bottles in the trunk of her car, I had a new plan to live a sober life. It was a month later that I stopped drinking for good. One day I didn't drink, and then I didn't drink the next day. I've now been sober for over three years. As for my fear of never drinking again for the rest of my life, I took a friend's advice. She said: "Give sobriety a try, and if you don't like it, you can always go back to drinking".

Every year on my AA birthday I reflect on whether I want to continue living a sober life, and every year so far I've made the decision to continue on my sober path. I know the AA motto is "one day at a time," and there are no guarantees that I won't relapse, but it's good for me to reflect on all the positive changes that have happened in my life as a result of sobriety. I know that I'm power-less over alcohol if I take a drink, but sobriety has given me a choice that I didn't have before. I'm no longer a slave to alcohol, and that is powerful.

Early sobriety wasn't easy. I felt lost without my connection to alcohol. Alcohol was my constant companion and best friend, even though it was slowly killing me. I had abandoned my friends, family and myself in order to keep drinking. When I faced the world in sobriety, I felt empty and alone. As a result, I had to learn how to connect with people and myself all over again – or perhaps for the first time. My motto in early sobriety was, "Just do the next right thing". That mantra motivated me to do the things that are part of a normal daily routine. It took a lot of energy just to take a shower in the morning, to eat and to go to bed at night. I didn't know how to do anything sober, so I talked to people at meetings, listened to their stories and just kept coming back.

In my quest to find out who I am as a sober person, I started gardening, took yoga, joined a meditation group and enrolled in a peer support training program. Even though I was meeting new people and doing things that I enjoyed, I still felt empty and like I didn't fit in. In order to stay sober, I needed to find a healthy way to manage my feelings of low self esteem and disconnection. I needed to find a spiritual connection to something outside of myself, or I was at risk for relapse. I first found this spiritual connection on a camping trip. I started taking photos of a chipmunk I'd befriended, and I was so lost in joy that I didn't feel the craving to drink.

Through Alcoholics Anonymous, I learned how to expand this connection I felt with animals to include a community of people who share my struggles with alcoholism. I've made some good friends and learned how to be a good friend in return. I learned how to listen, share and to be of service. I even learned how to pick up the phone and call someone before I take a drink. One thing I didn't know about AA meetings was that we laugh a lot, if I had known that it was fun to attend meetings, I might have gotten sober sooner.

I also went back to university. The first class I took was an introduction to Indigenous studies. I learned about Indigenous beliefs of living in concert with nature, and how everything is interconnected. I learned about ceremony and resilience. I went to a powwow, where I just cried for all the trauma that my ancestors had endured. However, I also felt like I didn't belong. I didn't know anything about the dances, the regalia or the protocols, so I decided to learn more. I continued going to community events. I asked Indigenous Elders for guidance on becoming more involved. Mostly, I just hung around, observed ceremonies, and copied what other people were doing. The first time I smudged, I felt a connection to something I can't fully understand. When I was surrounded by the smoke from the burning medicines, I felt a weight lift off my shoulders. It felt like going home to a place I'd never been before. I can't explain it – I just felt better.

I learned about the medicine wheel – another powerful tool that helps me maintain my sobriety. One interpretation of the medicine wheel is that it represents the four aspects of a person's well-being: spiritual, mental, physical and emotional. It can be used to find and maintain balance in one's life. AA meetings work on all of these aspects as well. For example, I physically have to leave the house to go to a meeting where I can share my emotions, learn from other's experiences and be part of a community.

Continuing on my journey to reconnect with my culture, I went to see a traditional Aboriginal counsellor. It was right before I left on a camping trip. After my counselling session, I had the most intensely spiritual moment of my life. Arriving at the campground as the sun was setting, I climbed a hill near the lake to make an offering and say a prayer. I said a prayer to the Great Spirit (a prayer on a flyer that I had picked up in lobby after meeting my counsellor). The prayer asked for strength and intelligence – not to conquer my enemies, but to fight the enemy within. I'd never seriously prayed before, and I'm still not sure that I believe in the Great Spirit, but the message was one that I could relate to.

I left an offering of berries by a tree stump and walked down a granite slab to the water's edge. I was alone, overlooking a quiet beach. I closed my eyes for a few minutes to meditate. When I opened them and looked across the water, a deer came out of the woods and stared right at me. I instantly felt a happiness that I had not felt in years. I was in awe, and crying tears of joy. Then another deer came out of the woods! I couldn't believe I was the only one there to see this. The deer were drinking from the lake, and one of them was playing with a frog. They were peaceful and carefree – two qualities that had been missing from my life since I quit drinking. It's difficult to describe, but those few minutes felt magical and life changing. I don't know if it was the result of the offering and prayer or just a coincidence, but I do know it was the most spiritual experience of my life. I also know that it never would have happened if I hadn't gotten sober. I had to become fully present in my life in order to experience that connection with nature, myself and my community.

5. Atheist in a Foxhole

Russ H.

On a sunny Saturday morning at the end of July, 1995, I pulled into the cul-de-sac where I lived with my wife of 19 years and our two teenage children. My sister's van was parked in the driveway. A police squad car occupied the spot in front of our house forcing me to park across the street. I don't recall how long I had been gone. It might have been a few hours or a few days. As I walked across the front yard I noticed that the van in the driveway was full of stuff – our stuff – and I wondered "are we going somewhere?" As I walked in the front door I was greeted by a police officer who asked me my name. The pivotal event that defines the end of the beginning of my AA story was about to unfold.

After identifying myself to him, the policeman told me that my wife and my sister were packing some things and would then be leaving with the children. He explained that he was there to make sure I didn't do anything to make this process any more difficult for them than it already was. I was instructed to take a seat in the nearest chair and stay there until my family was gone. The 28 years leading up to this moment are littered with countless incidents of blackout drinking and outrageous behavior – usually accompanied by negative consequences. The common thread through all of those years, the singular fact that drove me to my bottom, can be summed up neatly: having that police officer there that morning was a very good idea.

They left. I had no idea where they had gone. To reach my children I had to call my sister. She would then call them. If they felt like talking they would call me. Talking to my wife was not an option. I spent the rest of that weekend in miserable solitude mulling over a brand new realization. The way I was leading my life simply was not working. As so often mysteriously happens to alcoholics approaching their bottoms, I had acquired a Big Book and a schedule of AA meetings in my area. I had looked at them very briefly – just long enough to know that I was not interested in what they had to offer. Now, suddenly, there was a glimmer of interest in the meeting schedule. On Monday morning I called in sick and went down to a noon meeting at the nearest AA meeting place.

The Big Book tells us that "If you want what we have and are willing to go to any length to get it, then you are ready to take certain steps". The unsteady steps I took as I walked into that meeting were the first evidence of my readiness to go to any length. I had no expectations. I simply didn't know what else to do. I wound up going to three meetings that day.

I met people who said they were alcoholics and drug addicts. They told their stories and shared openly about what their lives had been like and what they were like now. I saw in them what it looks like when people like me stop drinking and using. I learned from them what it is like to speak frankly and without embarrassment about who we really are, what we have really done, how we really feel.

They allowed me to talk. They listened as I revealed anger, fear and shame and they were neither shocked nor disapproving. It dawned on me that I desperately needed to be with them. They were eager for me to join them. They didn't require anything from me other than my own willingness to belong. The friendship and love from those people, and others in the years that have followed, changed my life. At some point that day I realized that I wanted what those people had – to be a clean and sober person – more than I had ever wanted anything in my life. I had come to believe – not in God or spirituality – but simply that it really was possible for me to recover from alcoholism and drug addiction.

I got home late that evening. The hope and optimism I had felt while in the company of my new-found sober friends gave way to loneliness and desperation. Tears became weeping which became the convulsive sort of sobbing that makes it difficult to breathe and nearly impossible to speak. I found myself crying out "God help me. I don't know what to do. Show me what to do." Surprising words, perhaps, for an atheist to utter but that is what happened. They say there are no atheists in foxholes. I was in a metaphoric foxhole that evening. Apparently, not only are atheists sometimes in foxholes but some of us also sometimes pray.

The next morning I went in to work. I stopped first to speak to my boss. I told him that I was an alcoholic and drug addict. He was used to seeing me work long hours. I said I would now only be able to give him 40 hours per week – that my recovery had become my first priority. I thought there was a good chance I might be fired. Instead he looked at me and said "You look like a man who has had the weight of the world lifted from your shoulders. You have been a valuable asset here and we will stand by you now."

Next I visited his boss, a woman named Esther. I started to tell her the same story but I had hardly begun before she stopped me and said "Well, you probably should try to go to 90 meetings in 90 days. See if you can find a sponsor. I will try to get the company to cover the cost of a 30 day rehab. If they will you should do that." She sounded to me like she might be a recovered alcoholic herself although I learned later that day she was not. I was overcome with gratitude for the unconditional support I was receiving and told Esther I could hardly believe how wonderfully people were treating me that morning. She just shook her head and said "You expect too little from people". How true I now realize that was.

I left her office and went to my own. As I sat there, trying to maintain composure, my boss walked in and put a key to his house down on my desk. He said "Your wife and kids need your house more than you do. Come stay with me until you get back on your feet". I spent that night and the next several weeks accepting his generous offer. A few minutes later a coworker dropped by. News travels fast in a workplace where most people are housed in cubicles. She said she'd heard what was up and asked "So, you're a 12-Stepper?" Of course, I really wasn't but said I was. She smiled and said "Me too. Mine is a different '-A' but we use the same 12 Steps." Until then she had been a casual friend. That day she became a trusted confidant.

I left the office in time to make the 5:30 meeting near my home. When I arrived a man was waiting for me at the entrance to the room. He introduced himself as Scott, Esther's son. Scott was an alcoholic and addict who's "other" drug of choice was the same as mine. He had been clean and sober for 10 years and lived about six blocks down the road from me. Within a couple of weeks he became my first sponsor.

When I tell this story at AA meetings it is not uncommon for people to come up to me and say. "You're an atheist? How is that possible? You prayed for guidance and the very next day you did things you formerly would not have considered doing. Your prayer was answered. It may not have been a burning bush but what happened to you was surely a miracle." I'm inclined to agree that what happened feels miraculous. However, I simply do not believe in supernatural phenomena. When I hit my thumb with a hammer I am likely to cry out, "God damn it!" Driven to hopeless despair that evening I cried out "God help me!" The prayer was genuine but it was not a declaration of faith.

That marriage that seemed hopelessly doomed in July was reunited shortly before Christmas after a five month separation. I ecstatically shared my new and improved AA story which now featured restored domestic harmony and renewed family bonds. Then one day in early 2000 I returned from a two week business trip to learn that my wife had fallen in love with a friend of ours. For the first time as a sober man I was confronted with a devastating personal setback. It was not an easy time. I did not handle it gracefully. But I did share the experience with my sober friends. I let them see me suffer. Emotional pain has a tendency to rapidly morph into anger for me – even today – and my friends endured my anger too. As before, they did not turn away or express disapproval. I did not drink or use. Eventually the pain subsided. Life became, at first, tolerable then ultimately enjoyable once again.

I stayed clean and sober on the strength of the fellowship alone for over two years before I approached the 12 Steps with any real interest. It was then that I met the man who became my second AA sponsor. I have now known him for nearly 18 years. Although he will always be my sponsor, I no longer see him as a mentor. He is my trusted friend and one of the men in my life whom I love and know that I am loved by. He shared with me a point of view about life and recovery and AA that was, in large part, passed on to him by his sponsor. It is a point of view that resonates deeply with me and I pass it along to other men if they express an interest. It is not based on the 12 Steps as a recipe or formula for achieving sobriety.

The 12 Steps embody principles of a self-examined life that are neither unique nor new. They direct us to acknowledge who and what we are, to look for and rely upon help from outside ourselves, to examine past actions and motives, to understand that what we say and do may have greater or lesser merit, to seek to speak and act in ways that have greatest merit, to acknowledge our shortcomings, to make retribution for harm done to others whenever possible and to open our minds and hearts to great things we have not yet considered or felt. To adopt these goals (whether or not we try to achieve them specifically as prescribed in the 12 AA Steps) is a noble calling.

The notion that we should seek to speak and act in ways that have greatest merit implies that there is, in this world, an inherent morality. I believe this to be the case. Many AA members speak of seeking to do God's will. They are using different language based on a different world view but, it seems to me, they are saying essentially the same thing that I am saying. I have heard it said that there really is no "them" in AA. There is just "us." This applies to the whole world not just to AA.

What it's like now is a moving target. The ups and downs of being human have not been supplanted by some persistent state of happy and joyous freedom.

Sustaining long term sobriety is inevitably accompanied by growing older. Both processes seem, generally, to smooth rough edges and round off sharp corners. The emotional extremes of my drinking and using days have given way to the much less dramatic emotional extremes of life as a sober and recently retired person. More and more the virtues of "easy does it" and "live and let live" seem to be driving my daily existence.

Sometimes I wonder why I still call myself an alcoholic. The urge to drink or use drugs vanished entirely many years ago. An alcoholic, my thinking goes, is not someone who chooses to drink but, rather, someone who is unable to choose not to drink. By that definition I am now the opposite of alcoholic. Then I remember. "My name is Russ and I am an alcoholic" is by far the most powerful admission of my life. It was the first step of my journey into a life of sobriety. Today it continues to be the simple prelude to new friendships and astonishing experiences in Alcoholics Anonymous. It connects who I am now and what it is like now to who I was during those precious 28 years of drinking and using. Every one of those years and all the things that happened during them are bricks and mortar in the foundation of my life today.

6. Once a Sick Drug Addict

Patricia K.

I crawled into AA as a sick drug addict. At that time 12 step programs for my drug of choice did not exist in my area. It took me a number of years of sitting in the back of AA meetings and wondering if I belonged, to understand that I was indeed an alcoholic. I had the same disease that was being talked about in the literature and from the podium, I just happened to use other drugs as well as alcohol.

When I got to AA, I was emaciated and sick of body and heart. My use of alcohol and other drugs had rendered my 34 year old body into a knot of pain and tension that was held together by anger and resentment. I wore a black leather jacket and I had an attitude and a vocabulary to match; all meant to keep the world at bay. The reality was, I was terrified. My life up until that point had been full of abuse. Abused as a child, physically, sexually and mentally, I then become a mark for future abuse. To my mind the phrase "he hit me because he loves me", made sense. Before recovery I used any substance I could to numb the pain: alcohol, other drugs, men, food. It took years of step work and therapy to unravel all of this.

I first hit bottom during one of my many attempts to go university. Two of my classmates were in recovery in AA. Although I was drinking and using, I had a sense that we were kindred spirits. These two women listened to my horror stories of drinking and fights, and drug sickness. They came to the hospital when I had been beaten up by my ex-husband. One day, as I was going on about what a bastard my ex was, one of these women very gently said: "Do you think maybe you are the one with the problem?" I can still hear her voice. I started to attend AA meetings but was not convinced that I had a problem. I went to meetings drunk and high. I went to find a way to get HIM sober.

And then I had a moment of clarity. A street clinic doctor told me that I would soon die if I did not stop my destructive lifestyle. Lying on that hospital gurney and wanting nothing more than to get back to the drug that I had just overdosed on, the word powerless came to mind and I knew it was true. I admitted I was an alcoholic/addict. There was nothing divine about that occurrence. I had obviously heard what I needed to hear at the meetings I had attended even though I was under the influence.

Looking back at that young woman I was in early recovery I feel such empathy and respect for her. It was a struggle to understand life and to try to learn to accept my past and to believe that I could have a future in which I did not get beat up, I was not drug sick or hung over. Early on in my recovery, I accepted that I was an alcoholic/drug addict and that I could not safely use any mind altering substance.

However, I was tormented by pain, anger, shame and guilt for how I had lived my life, and I had yet to learn other ways to deal with these feelings. As a result, I didn't stay clean and sober right away. I had a number of one day relapses. However, I was taught to learn from those relapses. I was told to figure out if I was doing something that I shouldn't be, something that jeopardized my sobriety: an unhealthy relationship perhaps? I had to figure out what had caused me to relapse. Was I not dealing with the feelings that were surfacing now that I had stopped anesthetizing myself? Was I being honest? Going to meetings? Seeking the help and support I needed inside and outside AA? Was I trying to be of service? I had to grapple with these questions and figure out what I needed to do to stay clean and sober. There was no other entity earthbound or otherwise that was going to figure this out for me.

I was also grappling with the whole concept of god.

I am an atheist. I do not believe in god and yet I have remained sober in AA since Nov 9, 1986. Sober and attending a program that suggested that I could not get sober without a god.

I am one of those individuals who were told to "fake it till you make it" and I did that because I didn't want to die. I did try to find a god of my understanding. I prayed, even so far as to get on my knees to do so. But I could not believe in a god that would grant me sobriety if I asked in the right way. When I was nine months clean and sober, I returned to school to study Addictions and Mental Health and there were two nuns in my class. I would have long conversations with them about the nature of spirituality and religion.

It didn't help... I still did not believe.

However I continued to attend meetings of AA and other 12 step programs and I am very thankful for the support that I received there. I read the Big Book and took some very good guidance from what I read. I did however change my copy so that "He" was taken out of the text. Later the term "God" was taken out. I used a paper clip to contain parts of the book such as the chapter "To Wives" because I found it to be sexist and codependent. I figured it was my book, it was my sobriety and I would do what I needed to stay sober and fairly sane.

It is only in the last 10 years that I have come out as an atheist in AA. At first, I began to speak tentatively of my non-belief. I wanted to tell the truth and I thought there may be others who needed to hear that I do not believe in any god, but I was nervous. And rightly so. I did get flak from some quarters. It was even suggest by one person that perhaps I am not an alcoholic after all, if I could remain sober without god.

However I also got encouragement and even thanks for sharing my non beliefs and the fact that I had remained clean/sober for 20 + years without god.

About five years ago, I was told that an Agnostic, Atheists and Free Thinkers group had been started in my area. At first, I was reluctant to attend. Even after many years of sobriety, I remembered what my life was like before I found the 12 step fellowships and I remembered the struggle to gain and maintain sobriety and I did not want to jeopardize my sobriety. Even though I did not believe in god and I did question much of the dogma of the program, mainstream AA and other 12 step programs had been my reed and I was afraid to let go. However, curiosity got the best of me and I finally went to a meeting of Beyond Belief.

Far from jeopardizing my sobriety, attending Agnostic, Atheists and Free Thinkers meetings has deepened and enhanced my sobriety. I found acceptance for the non-believer that I was. No one was going to try to convert me or, worse, question my sobriety because I did not believe in god. In the Agnostic, Atheist and Free Thinkers meetings I didn't have to pretend to believe in something I did not. I did not have to deny that I believe that I am solely responsibility for my sobriety. It is up to me to figure out what to do to remain sober and then do it. Of course I am not doing this alone. I have had and continue to have great teachers and support in the fellowship.

And it has worked so far. Using the tools that I had picked up in 12 step programs, I have remained sober through the deaths of both of my parents. Relationships and jobs have come and gone. There have been financial and health difficulties but still have had not had to drink or do drugs.

My life is far from perfect but it is so much more than I ever believed I could have. I deal with depression and PTSD every day. When I was nine years clean I was suicidal and so I finally took the advice of my doctor and started to take medication. Her words "it will give you an opportunity to get a foot hold on life". Many years of therapy and 12 step work later, I am now not on medication. However, I would have no qualms about going on a medication with the consultation of my doctors if I felt it necessary.

Although I still have these "issues" in my life, today I have a rich full life. I finally finished university. I have a good job that I enjoy. I am not wealthy but the bills are paid. I found my creativity. I found my love of nature and the joy in being outside. I am a tree hugger. The biggest payoff for me in staying clean and sober is the respect I have for myself today. I can look in the mirror and know that I have not deliberately harmed another person today. Although the wording of the original 12 steps is archaic and Christian-based, digging down, I found the essence of each step, the principle it is based on. These are my creed for living.

In the Twelve and Twelve it states, "Of course, we were glad that good home and religious training had given us certain values". Coming from an abusive and dysfunctional family I did not have that kind of education. The only values I learnt as a child were the value of a "26er" and the value of a good lie to keep from being beaten or abused. My religious education consisted of me being sent to stand outside the classroom because I would not accept some nonsense the nuns were trying to feed me.

I do not mean to sound bitter, so forgive me if I do. I am not. I honestly believe in what the late, great John Lennon said, "Whatever gets you through the night". I am happy for believers and wish them well. I hope there is room for all of us in Alcoholics Anonymous, believers and non-believers alike.

7. The Beginning

Brent P.

In returning to AA In 2010, broke and briefly homeless, I had already decided, before someone made the point by asking, "so what are you going to do differently this time?", that I indeed had to change my attitude to AA.

After 27 years of toying with the program I knew that one more flagrant, arrogant FU from me to AA, spelled the end. It's only in AA that so many stories begin with, "The End", and, if fortunate, end with, "The Beginning".

The End

An alcoholic addicted to opiates and crack cocaine, I had fulfilled two of the three prognostications promised to alcoholics if they continued to drink: institutions, jail and/or death. You can figure out the one I've eluded so far.

Nevertheless I knew what it meant to be a "shivering denizen" of King Alcohol's dark realm. I had experienced those last 10 to 15 years of absolute horror. The ominous, apocalyptic sound of the Four Horsemen's mounts, their hooves pounding relentlessly with grim determination, shot electric fear through every nerve in my body.

What I had come to believe was my last stab at AA began when I came out of an institution that treats alcoholics. A hospital that medically detoxed me then put me into a program that fundamentally told me a lot of what I already knew. My brain was damaged as was my liver. The degree to which either would repair themselves was entirely up to me and my constitution. But the real message was, stop assuming that you're at the head of the class, shut up and take seriously what others can tell you about alcoholism and addiction, whether doctors or peers in AA.

After seven weeks of balanced meals, exercise, massage, acupuncture, art therapy, doctor's lectures, group therapy and other things I can't remember, I was polished, dressed up and pushed out the door. They'd done all they could, including suggesting I start attending AA meetings (again!). ASAP.

There were a few days of sleeping on a friend's couch before I secured a small bachelor's apartment.

Now, I wonder, have I painted my self portrait clearly enough that you can picture me in your mind? Low bottom drunk/drug addict with a high opinion of himself. Dirty, rough looking, someone you'd hurry past on the sidewalk?

If that's what you imagine, you wouldn't be too far off the mark.

However it only took three of those 27 years to arrive at that station. The previous twenty four years I was a successful advertising copywriter. I traveled to some of the world's most exotic locations, with a hefty expense account, to make commercials. Commercials!

Though not rich I was at the upper end of the wage scale. I had a salary that allowed me to buy and sell – one at a time – a 3 story building that was renovated to the nth degree, two houses in a very desirable downtown neighborhoods and, finally, a condo that was one of 17 unique units in what had once been a carpet factory.

I moved there shortly after an embarrassing incident cost me my partnership in a start-up agency. Or almost did. Since our partnership agreement was still to be completed, the other two partners had no basis upon which to sever me from the partnership. Nevertheless they wanted me gone. Some sort of arrangement would have to be crafted. Basically it would involve them paying me to stop showing up there.

I was in a rehab when the negotiating began. I left it to my brother to act for me. He happened to be the CEO and one of three senior partners in a sizeable law firm. That he was also a chartered accountant meant I had formidable representation. My brother and the accountant who was representing my partners, settled on a low six figure payout.

I won again, or so it appeared. Back in charge of my own life I decided I could take six months off; rest, recuperate, then like Lazarus, rise to take the job market by storm. I had to pause to admire my fine work! I was already calculating what a spectacular financial year it was going to be. Double the amount I'd settled for and that's what my salary would be. Easy Street would be my address once again.

There was a recession and advertising agencies couldn't afford much more than one senior guy like me and he/she was usually the creative director. While I thought I was perfectly cut out to be a creative director, nobody else appeared to share that confidence. My reputation had changed from one of a young, clever, big picture copywriter, to serious drunk, who looked and smelled the part. If you got me on a run of good days, then you were lucky; a run of bad days and anything could happen. I once passed out in an important meeting, my face dropping, slowly at first then more rapidly, until it was flat on the boardroom table. That ground the meeting to a halt while I was removed.

When I won that payout from my former partners, I didn't realize that was it for me in the advertising business.

Fast forward a few years, after I'd been robbed by masked, armed crack-heads, been ripped off for $13,000 in a set up dope deal and repeatedly seen the most nightmarish side of humanity, I knew it was time to get out of Dodge. So I sold my condo and moved to an apartment in one of the city's nicer neighborhoods. With the cash from the condo I could buy drugs and booze by the bundle and not have to leave the apartment for days.

I lived that way for about a year and I knew my brain was not functioning properly, that the tiny strokes that occur in your brain every time you smoke crack, were catching up to me. That every time I smoked crack I could have a sudden, crippling stroke. The alcohol I needed to accompany every crack-isode was so that I didn't go into a major panic attack and bite my tongue off, was burning through the lining of my stomach. I was mixing vodka with Pepto Bismol and still my stomach burned and stung like I'd swallowed a swarm of bees. Finally, what started out as an occasional thing to help me sleep, opiates were required every day in greater and greater amounts. So when my brother finally caught up with me and said, "you need help", I wrapped my arms around his waist – I was sitting and he was standing – buried my head just below his chest and let go with great heaving sobs.

So what are you going to do differently this time?

I was just over seven or eight weeks sober and still in a complete fog. Work wasn't an issue since I didn't have any nor could I have done any. I went primarily to daytime meetings and usually just sat there. On one of those occasions I thought to myself, "This is what you do all the time. Once you start feeling better you become argumentative, challenging the crap that inevitably drives you nuts. Then when you feel like you're back to normal, you tell yourself you can't take anymore of the nonsense and you stop coming".

That was something I could do differently. The next change was a deal I made with myself; I could say anything I wanted in AA as long as it wasn't driven by anger, wasn't meant to be provocative nor could it be hurtful. Sure, it sounded good but could I do it? Turned out, with a little practice, I could. In fact with the nonsense I found amusing ways to show it for what it was.

It took awhile but I joined that group and pitched in all I could. It wasn't until six months that you could chair a meeting so that kept being held out to me as a carrot. What they didn't know was that I had severe anxiety accompanied by panic; the very last thing I wanted to do was chair a meeting. Rather than let that drive me out, as it had in the past (without knowing it part of my drinking and using was me self medicating), I decided I needed some outside help.

I finally ended up with two doctors, remarkable men whose compassion was equaled only by their BS detectors. I was prescribed a mild tranquilizer to use only in the most extreme cases (I only had a few pills at any time) and I was taught how to relax. Relaxing is a skill that you have to practice before you can really use it. But I practiced and if I still couldn't halt the anxiety in a critical (to me) circumstance, I had the medication as back up.

I had dealt with two of the things that could make me walk out of a meeting, but there was another that had been a deal breaker so many times in the past – God and all the Judeo Christian constructs that infused many of the meetings. Add to that a Big Book that hadn't changed in 75 years – I think it still refers to wives as "the little woman" – a book that people read and re-read as if there were treasure buried deep in its pages.

It was then somebody suggested I checkout AA Agnostica. I was suspicious. But I returned several times and finally wrote a kind of harsh rebuttal to one of the articles that appear fresh and new every week. I was thanked for my opinion.

In fact I was invited to contribute some articles to the site. And as happy as I felt I could be in my regular AA group, I was growing more and more connected to this movement that became noticed here by virtue of an Intergroup hearing and ruling that would determine if secular groups in Toronto could be listed. They couldn't. But that didn't seem to impede the progress of AA Agnostica. The website flourishes as many are drawn to it and, for the first time, an atmosphere of open mindedness – not the kind that means turning off your critical faculties so you can accept a fairy tale as the reason for your sobriety – but instead the kind that encourages new ideas while caring little or nothing for your religion. AA Agnostica, the website, is a barometer of the movement around the world while bringing hope to people who either had to keep their thoughts to themselves or often live with them bottled up. The optimism the site exudes is palpable and compelling, telling this alcoholic, AA is changing and one day, in the not too distant future, the secular meetings and their members will be leading the charge to an AA that enjoys a symbiotic relationship with Science & Medicine, Mental & Physical Health Facilities and much more.

So I thank AAAA and AA Agnostica for giving me the hope I'm not certain I ever had. And I thank AA for its groundbreaking work and the vital insight it brought to treating that most acute symptom every alcoholic struggles with, loneliness. AA is a real community that AAAA continues to learn from and show gratitude towards.

Despite the fact that I'm still broke and on a disability pension that barely covers my monthly costs, I'm happy. I have inside help and I have outside help. My current doctor is a member of AA herself and actively involved in the science of addiction.

And for the first time in my life I wake up almost every morning now and on the cinema screen in my head I see, in a fantastic font, the words I've so desperately wanted to see at the introduction to my story:

The Beginning

8. A Programme of Honesty?

Suzanne M.

My name is Suzanne. I am an atheist alcoholic. I came into AA at 54 years old – totally worn-down after 37 years of drinking. I chose my first group because it was only a short walk from where I lived. It had a strong Christian ethic and – as I now realise – a very fundamentalist approach to the programme. They even included the Lord's Prayer at meetings, which is most unusual in the UK. After six weeks of attending those meetings I was still sober (good) but found that meetings were like a dose of unpleasant medicine (bad) so I switched to another group. I chose this next group because, again, it was only a short walk – in the other direction – from my home. Astonishingly, this meeting, too, had the Lord's Prayer. A freakish coincidence.

With the Serenity Prayer and the Lord's Prayer in the same meeting I felt that something was wrong, but that I should keep quiet about it. I can't say that I was aggressively atheist at the time. The Christian faith does not play a large part in the everyday life of most Brits so we are hardly ever required to express an opinion on it. It just seemed very strange that it was thrusting itself into my consciousness in my new venture of AA meetings. The references to "God", "He" and "Him" felt like a strange throwback to the unthinking acceptance of Christian mythology of my childhood Sunday School days.

Strangely though, someone at that meeting introduced me to the Richard Dawkins book *The God Delusion*. Reading that was a light bulb moment. I switched groups again, and found one – walking distance again – which included an openly atheist member! This was progress. But I must say that, although I was beginning to think the unthinkable myself, there was always the very frightening and overwhelmingly loud voice of many people in the fellowship who would tell me it was wrong to go behind the text of the Big Book or to question what it meant. Also that it was wrong to question why we say prayers to God in meetings or why the Big Book constantly refers to God. And the punch line was always, "If you continue to question the programme in that way, you will drink again." People would say "It's a programme of honesty" but they would also say – bizarrely – "Fake it to make it". I feel very uncomfortable faking a belief that a magical father-figure was managing my sobriety.

I tried for a long time to just keep my mouth shut in the face of people insisting that the words of the Big Book are inviolable and that we should not probe behind their meaning or teachings. But the rebel in me comes out once a year when I do my birthday share at my present home group. I feel that on that occasion I am allowed to express my honest opinion about how I got sobriety and how I keep it. What I say is that, for me, AA is as good as the people who are in it. It is the human fellowship of AA that keeps me sober. I can find no evidence, in my sobriety, of an interfering god who has played a part in it.

So last year, seven years into sobriety, and always with a nagging doubt lurking in my mind that there was something not quite right, or not quite honest, about my sobriety, I decided to be brave (or to put my sobriety at risk, as I was darkly warned) and work out what I really could accept from the Big Book and the programme, and what I could leave. I looked at the AA Agnostica website for the first time, and it was a breath of fresh air. People were confidently, and rationally, saying there things which I did not dare to utter because of the power of the BB Taliban. It is strange – Christian overtones are not unduly burdensome in most UK meetings (or maybe I, like many others, have learned to zone-out when they arise). But I personally class religious beliefs alongside fairy stories, and I feel uncomfortable when fairy-stories and superstition are peddled as being an essential part of recovery. I have occasionally wondered what would happen if I announced at a meeting that it was the fairies who kept me sober. Would people respect my belief?

It is a delicate balance. Neither I nor other non-believers want to bring down AA. I know that it is AA, not Smart Recovery or any other similar structure that keeps me sober. AA works for me. But I worry for the next generation of alcoholics. In my early days I read the Big Book four times in a short period, hoping that it would transfer itself into my brain by osmosis and make me sober. I had misgivings about the tone of condescension toward women and non-Christians, and about the dated language and images, but mostly about the overtly Christian tone of the text. Yet it has taken me seven years to find my own voice and my confidence to challenge the prevailing dogma. People ask why most newcomers attend one meeting and never come back. Possibly it is because they are just not ready for it. But I also guess that the sight of all those references to God in the 12 Step wall–hanging, together with the references to God in the readings, are enough to make many newcomers think they have stumbled into a cult and so they run away.

As I write this I am in the process of setting up a Freethinkers/Atheist group in my home town in the UK. There are only four or five such groups in the whole of the UK, as far as I can tell. I want a group where people, newcomers especially, can speak truthfully about their interpretation of the AA programme. I want AA to adapt, modernise and survive. People look pityingly at me when I raise these issues – they seem to suggest that I am making this fuss because I am angry or afraid. I have given it a lot of thought. I find that the discomfort I feel in quietly acquiescing to something I think is false is in itself a disturbance to my sobriety.

I hope, when the new group starts, that AA in the UK can tolerate a tiny wind of change.

9. A Friend of Jim B.

Alex M.

When I was a small boy the neighborhood kids would gather on weekends to play kickball. We would all line up eagerly waiting to hear our name called for each team. I would look down at the ground and shuffle my feet knowing once again my name would the last one spoken. That was the start of a lifetime of not fitting in.

Raised as an only child in Kentucky during the 1950s, my father worked as a chemical engineer while my mother spoiled me at home. Food, clothing and shelter were easily provided. Our neighborhood was safe enough to leave our doors unlocked. Stay at home moms watched over each other's kids so we never got into too much trouble. On Halloween we roamed far and wide, filling our sacks till they overflowed. At Christmas entire families went caroling house to house.

The only advice I remember getting from my father was to work hard, never ask for anything from anybody, get the best education I could and find a good job. My mother taught me that it didn't matter who I thought I was or what I felt; all that mattered was how I appeared to the world. Keep your mouth shut, control your emotions, trust no one, and hold your secrets close. Lying to myself and pretending with others became routine.

When my father drank he turned into an angry, combative alcoholic who terrified me and abused my mother. As his life became more unmanageable our lives became more unmanageable.

I lived in fear of my father's rages and not knowing when my mother would grab me up to flee the house during yet another domestic quarrel. All I wanted was to escape the chaos. At an early age I discovered books. I would hide in my room and read. Reading took me to a safe place, but it was empty and lonely.

Down deep I yearned to be part of something more. A lot more. Like Bill W., I wanted to prove to the world I was important. I wanted to fit in with others, be accepted and be the big-shot. I wanted the world to do my bidding and when it didn't I got angry. The first resentment I remember was when the bully next door hit me with a sucker punch when I was five. I got even and remember his name to this day.

Going through school I tried to fit in with various groups. There were the usual Nerds, Jocks, Scholars and Romeos. None welcomed me. After a while I found a few outcasts who spent their time drinking. An unpopular group, they stayed in the shadows. Since I had recently discovered bourbon would help me sleep at night and ease my worries during the day, I joined the group. In no time those misfits became my friends and I worked to become the best drinker around. At last I fit in.

In high school I developed an interest in medicine and I decided I was going to become a doctor. I knew it would take many years of schooling and hard work but I felt it was a worthy goal and might even relieve some of the turmoil in my life.

Somehow I was able to balance drinking and schooling long enough to enter a fine college in Philadelphia where I was on my own for the first time. Recurrent blackouts that started during freshman year terrified me, but instead of addressing the cause I denied there was a problem.

As my college drinking progressed my grades worsened but my desire to become a physician overcame my desire to drink. As a hard drinker, I was able to cut down on the alcohol and graduated with honors.

During medical school and later training I continued to drink when off duty but was too busy to drink while working. Once in medical practice, like Dr. Bob, I felt an obligation never to drink while working with patients but drank to oblivion when not at work.

During my early professional years I got married and later divorced. When I asked my wife why she wanted a divorce she said it was because I was never there for her. She was right. All I did was work and get drunk. It was all about me.

Several years after my divorce, I met and married an exceptional lady from my hometown. Shortly after our honeymoon she was diagnosed with cancer and died within a few months.

The night she died I went outdoors and noticed that three white jet contrails had formed a perfect triangle in the sky. For some reason that image reminded me of the Holy Trinity. Believing God was mocking the death of my wife, I ran around screaming and cursing at the sky. I never set foot in a church again.

From that point on I used my wife's death as justification to become even more selfish and self-centered. I drank with impunity. I just didn't care anymore. I left practice and took a medical administrative position. Somehow I managed to remain employed but my drinking progressed over the next ten years. I drifted from desk job to desk job where it was easier for me to drink without consequence. By the time I reached my early fifties I owned my own medical consulting business which allowed me to drink however I wanted.

Through those years I had acquired a third wife who no longer wanted to be around me and a family that I had pushed aside. Eventually I stopped working completely because work continued to interfere with my drinking. The more I drank the worse I felt. I saw no way out of my inability to live sober or my disgust at living drunk. Suicide beckoned, and I would line up shotgun shells on the table by my bed praying to have the courage to load the gun and use it. By then my life consisted of sitting on a couch yelling at nameless newscasters on TV while drinking from blackout to blackout.

One day a friend offered to take me to an AA meeting and I agreed, probably because I was still drunk. All I remember from that meeting was that folks told me to ask God for help not drinking one day at a time and to keep coming back.

I had no problem accepting that I was an alcoholic, but I had a big problem with the default AA solution: God. Despite being raised in the church, I never felt a personal connection to any God or religion that crossed my path. No Higher Power ever manipulated my life. There was no heaven or hell. Death was final. Events were governed by the laws of nature and coincidences were not arranged by God. Even when in the depths of my pain I had never cried out "God help me". I had no idea if there was or was not a God, and really didn't care. I was an agnostic for sure and probably an atheist at heart.

I had repeatedly demonstrated that my own will-power and self-reliance could not get me sober, and I needed to find something to get and stay sober. Lack of power over alcohol: that was my dilemma.

Then I discovered what became for me the five most important words in AA, as we know it today – "God as we understood him". The words "as we understood him" were added to the Steps as a result of the work of Jim B., one of the very first atheists in AA. And those few words saved my life because they allowed me to turn to a spiritual power of my own understanding for help. I no longer had to rely on a religious power of someone else's understanding.

In "Working With Others" Bill says, "If the man be agnostic or atheist, make it emphatic that he does not have to agree with your conception of God. He can choose any conception he likes, provided it makes sense to him. The main thing is that he be willing to believe in a power greater than himself and that he live by spiritual principles". (BB, p. 93)

My responsibility today is to carry the message of hope and recovery to another alcoholic who still suffers. To be effective I must put aside my personal frustration that the Big Book not so subtly preaches that the highest Higher Power available to alcoholics is the traditional Christian God. This is not really surprising, given the influence of the Protestant Oxford Group in the early growth of AA.

So I got out pen and paper and wrote down what the "God of my understanding" looked like. In no way did it resemble the God of my upbringing, but it was a power that I could turn to for strength, direction, and guidance as I went through each day trying to do the next right thing.

But what could I replace God with? Would it be Willingness, or Honesty, or Open-Mindedness, or Group of Drunks, or Home-group, or Sponsor, or Allah, or Confucius, or Buddha, or Great Spirit, or the Cosmos, or Nature, or Love, or Compassion, or Tolerance or Service?

I needed some kind of power in my life by which I could not only stay sober but also find a new way of living. I couldn't rely entirely on the power of my own self-will or self-reliance, since that approach had failed completely. So I had to find some other power of my understanding by which I could live. That power was to be mine, and mine alone. No longer need I feel intimidated by anyone else's Higher Power that was discussed in the rooms of AA.

The power I draw on today comes from the feeling I get deep within me when I look up at the stars and realize that somehow all of us in this universe are connected. I am not connected by choice or by some imaginary divine hand. I am connected by the collective power of Love, Goodness and Compassion. In AA terms these spiritual principles are "the God of my understanding".

My power is not a heavenly power; it is a human power. It is not a power created by my self-will; it simply exists because I exist. This is the power I turn to for strength, hope and direction in my life, rather than the power of John Barleycorn.

I feel my power most when I am in the rooms of AA and working one-on-one with other alcoholics. I especially like working with alcoholics struggling with the "God bit", as Jim B. put it, since I can share my story and be living proof that any of us can get sober, including those who struggle with their own concept of religion, God, Higher Power or spirituality.

Today I am grateful that Bill W. created AA, but I am so much more grateful for his fellow alcoholics Jim B., Hank P. and others who ensured AA could provide not only for believers, but also for non-believers like myself. Certainly, more needs to be done to further "widen the gateway" of our fellowship, but that's a story for another day.

10. My Name is Joan

Joan C.

My name is Joan and I am an alcoholic. I am an agnostic and my home group is "We Agnostics" on the island of Maui. I recently celebrated 46 years of sobriety in Alcoholics Anonymous.

I was born 81 years ago in St. Louis, Missouri. I like to say that I was born and raised a freethinker but that only applies to the first ten years of my life. My father was a very intelligent man – and an atheist. I once asked him about churches and he explained that there were many different churches with many different ideas and that if I ever found one whose beliefs I agreed with I should join – otherwise I probably wouldn't want to belong to something I didn't believe in.

Everything changed when I was 10 years old. My father died of spinal meningitis. My mother's mother came swooping in from California and convinced my mother that that was god's punishment for not raising us as Catholics. We moved to California and I was sent to St Mary's Academy, a private girl's school, where I was a fish out of water. I tried to fit in – I tried to believe. I even erected an altar in my bedroom and said the Rosary over and over but I had many doubts.

Looking back I realize that I was a very disturbed child. I hated California and wanted my father to come back.

I acted out by refusing to do homework, breaking every rule that I could and spent a lot of time in Sister Josephine's office.

In the 10th grade I was expelled. And I gave up any idea of being a Catholic. My doubts won.

I discovered alcohol when I was 13 or 14. I was introduced to Tom Collins by a woman for whom I babysat. I liked the feeling it gave me from the start – I was kind of out of myself. I remember the first glass or two and then my next memory is of my head in the toilet – very, very sick.

For the next few teenage years I attended public school – when I felt like attending – and did a lot of drinking. My poor mother had no control over me.

I quit school in the eleventh grade and I managed to get a job as a telephone operator. I worked and partied and lived at home for a year or two until I became pregnant and married my first husband. He had been drafted into the army and eventually was sent to Korea for a short stint and I went back to Los Angeles to stay with his parents. I was pregnant with our second child – the daughters were one year and three days apart. I was to go on to have four children – the fourth was born a few days before my 24th birthday. I decided I would like to have 12 children.

While staying with my in-laws I was introduced to the Big Book of Alcoholics Anonymous. My father in law was an alcoholic – died of alcoholism – and at one point had called AA. He said that two men called on him and left the book. Being a compulsive reader I read it and even as a teenager there was parts I could relate to.

I realize now that I never was a social drinker. I never wanted one drink. Even as a teenage I would turn down drinks if there wasn't going to be enough to get drunk.

My husband returned from Korea. As time went on our marriage, not too sound to begin with, really began to fall apart. He started staying out all night – "drinking with the boys" – and denied having other women. I was becoming more and more distressed and depressed. And then I found I was pregnant again.

I knew that mentally there was no way that I could go through another pregnancy with the marriage being the way it was. I called a mutual friend and begged him to tell me the truth and he said that yes, there definitely was another woman. When I confronted my husband with this fact, he informed me that he didn't want a divorce but was going to continue seeing her. What he said to me was, "you're pregnant and you have four children – there's nothing you can do about it". I knew then that it was over. I was thirty years old with four children and even if I had to take the children and go sleep in the park it was over.

I forged his name on a check made out to him and cashed it and started making phone calls. Abortions were illegal then but I finally found a woman from East Los Angeles who was willing to perform it. She came to the house with a coat hanger and a catheter and tried to abort me. It was not successful and she had to return a second time. She didn't even wash her hands – nothing was sterilized – and I developed a terrible infection. Several months later – I hadn't aborted the fetus – I started to hemorrhage and was taken to the hospital. Eventually they took me to the operating room and did a D&C. A year later I had my uterus removed.

I was now a single woman in my thirties. I drank a lot. I also had a pill problem. Amphetamines were readily available in the 50s and 60s. All you had to do was call the doctor, tell him you wanted to lose a few pounds and he would call in the prescription to the local pharmacy.

I didn't drink much at home – I was a bar drinker. As my drinking increased I would be away from home several days at a time. I had a friend who would stop in with groceries and to check on the children. I knew it was just a matter of time before child welfare would appear on the scene and put the children in foster homes.

I woke up one morning terribly sick – bed wet – hands shaking – looked in the mirror and saw what a mess I was. I was so very depressed. I knew that I was an alcoholic and had to stop drinking but I didn't know how I could live without alcohol. My life seemed a hopeless, unbearable mess and I wanted to die. I knew that if I committed suicide that the children would end up in foster homes. I rationalized in my sick mind that if I could live another five years they would be older and better able to get along on their own. I was 35 years old and planned to wait until I was 40 – and I would do it then.

I went to my first AA meeting on October 5, 1968 and my whole world changed.

I knew that AA helped alcoholics stop drinking but I was very concerned when I attended my first meeting. There was something about turning your life over to god and a lot of other god words in "How it works". If this was some kind of a religion I knew it wasn't going to work for me. When the meeting was over a couple of people came over to me and I expressed my concerns about the god thing. I was told that I should just ignore that. The old "take what you can use and leave the rest".

I didn't want to find God – I wanted to find out how to live in this miserable world without drinking. I knew I was an alcoholic and I knew I had to quit drinking. I was uncomfortable with the praying and the hand holding – it was something that made me feel apart from the other members. It was the same feeling I had in St. Mary's Academy. I was told the old "fake it til you make it" but for me it just didn't take.

However, time went by and indeed things did get better. I got my high school diploma by passing a GED test and that was enough to get me into the nursing program and to become a Licensed Vocational Nurse.

I attended many meetings in the beginning years – the first year I went every day. I was very active in Twelfth Step work, answered phones in Central Office, took my turn as Secretary of different meetings and – yes – washed ash trays and coffee cups. When I came in, where I came in, there wasn't all that much talk of god and miracles. Most people credited a god with their sobriety but in the discussions the talk was more of sober living.

Gradually over the years there were changes in the meetings. More and more the talk was of miracles from above and less of one's own efforts to cope with life's problems.

The only problem I had was that I was still an agnostic.

I met my second husband toward the end of my first year of sobriety. We dated for a few years and finally married. He and I were both 42 years of age when he had a heart attack and died.

When I had been sober ten years, I met my last husband, Bill, who had twenty years of sobriety. Bill and I dated and a few years later were married. He bought a condo on Maui as an investment. We both loved Maui and when he retired we sold the condo, bought a house and moved over here. We were married 25 years. Bill passed away in 2004.

After 30 some years of sobriety I just gave up meetings.

I got so I was only attending on special days and I did make a point of attending once a year on my birthday. We have a pretty large meeting on Maui called "Kihei Morning Serenity" – KMS for short and they gave chips. So for some years I would attend that meeting to accept my chip. When I gave my little talk I would tell them that I was an unbeliever. I would encourage anyone who was a believer to pray and do whatever it took to stay sober but that if they were atheists or agnostics to know that the program would work for them. I was very concerned about the number of people who were turned off by all the god talk and weren't coming back to the meetings. So often I heard them say that they were told that they couldn't stay sober if they didn't find god. I would say that if anyone tried to tell them that you can't stay sober without god, ask them, "What about Joan?" By then I had probably more years of sobriety than anyone else on the island. Usually, when the meeting was over, several people would come up to me and whisper that they were non-believers too. I think of them as closet atheists.

For some years I have been the AA liaison for the prison – Maui Community Correctional Center. About nine years ago I discovered that no one was taking meetings into the women's prison. I went in to the prison for a week or two to set up meetings and realized I was going in by myself. Looking back I am surprised I got away with it – you are supposed to be certified to go in – background check, etc. Eventually I rounded up enough volunteers so that the meetings were held on on a regular basis. I am happy to say that we are going on the 10th year and haven't missed a single Wednesday night.

I told an AA friend, "If you ever come across anyone who is having trouble with the religious aspects of the program, let me know and I will talk to him or her". One day he called to tell me about a newcomer – Rich – who was an atheist. He invited me over to dinner and that is when I met Rich.

We became friends and talked about starting a meeting for nonbelievers. Rich discovered that there were "We Agnostics" meetings on the mainland that were recognized in New York and we were on our way.

We started out being listed as "We Agnostics – non religious format" – but there were howls of protest from the AA community – "This is not a religious program!" So Rich changed it to read "We Agnostics – no prayers" and that worked. Our first meeting was on July 27, 2006. As time went on more and more people were coming to the meetings.

When some vandals burned down the Bridge Club where our meetings were held, we moved outside to the adjacent park. There is a beautiful Flower Tree and we all bring folding chairs and have our meeting under this beautiful tree. It was pictured on the front page of the Grapevine a year or so ago.

We now have three "We Agnostics" meetings a week and have anywhere from ten or fifteen people to thirty per meeting. We plan to start a fourth meeting when the Bridge Club is rebuilt.

I left AA because I am a non-believer and became more and more uncomfortable in the meetings with all the god talk and talk of leaving everything in god's hands – frankly superstitious gobbledy-gook. I am back because we now have meetings – We Agnostic meetings – where I finally feel like I belong.

Today I have a wonderful life. I have always been active in volunteer work in and out of AA. I have friends. I play Bridge. My health is good. Sometimes I look around and wonder, "How did you get from there to here?" In all my years of sobriety I have never felt as close and as much a part of Alcoholics Anonymous as I do since we have We Agnostics meetings.

New We Agnostic AA meetings are springing up all over the world. We are in the midst of great changes and now have a wonderful opportunity to offer help to all suffering alcoholics, including agnostics, atheists and all other nonbelievers.

11. Spirituality As I Understand It

Gabe S.

I showed signs of what I think of as "spiritual malady" from as far back as I can remember.

As a child, I was absorbed in fantasy. I was the God of my own fantasies, creating worlds at will. In those worlds I was whatever I fancied: a great warrior, or footballer, or rock guitarist. Often I was a superhero. I fantasized because I was not happy to be who I really was in the world as it really was.

The ambient world was actually very good to me. My family was well off and we lived in a leafy, desirable part of London. My parents were loving and kind and very liberal. But they did not let just anything go and taught me right from wrong. I have two much older brothers. One was nice enough, though a bit distant. The other was loving. They were (and still are) extremely successful at pretty much whatever they do: top of the class, head of school, best at sports and so on. The loving brother often played games with me. He always won. My mother from time to time voiced the view that, in this way or that, I would never be as good as them. I felt very inadequate. For some reason, when I was six, I was sent to a psychoanalyst who told me that I wanted to kill my brothers and my parents. I think that as a result of this, I felt that I was horrible inside. I was the worst of possible beings. I carried a terrible secret.

Growing up (or rather failing to do so) in the 1960s, the hippy-drug culture was all around. At about seven, the idea of taking drugs took root. Drugs represented an escape from reality, and an alternative lifestyle that appealed greatly. I went into denial even then. There was plenty of publicity that I saw and heard, saying: "Drugs are dangerous. They can ruin your life or kill you. You could become an "addict". "Don't do them!" This had no effect on my thinking. I had no fear. I began inhaling solvents at about ten. Then, aged fourteen, I started smoking marijuana. I quickly became a daily user and a true addict, with craving and obsession. I took whatever drugs I could find and afford.

I left home at sixteen, went to live in a squat and pursue the hippy lifestyle. I remember one time I took some LSD and went to a park. I tried hard to be at one with the beautiful flowers.

I got bored with drugs and with the hippy life and lucked my way into a good university. I received scholarships for a Master's and then a PhD. I excelled. My confidence grew along with my self-esteem. But however much I acheived, it was not enough. Inside I was always inadequate.

I coped with some of my inner violence by training hard at Kung Fu. I enjoyed the aesthetic qualities, the endorphin high, the fighting and smashing things. I became skilled, tough and physically confident. Inside I remained inadequate.

I had always liked drinking and, as soon as I stopped the drugs, I began to drink more. I drank nearly every day for about thirty years. A lot. I liked drinking. I am sociable and always found heavy drinkers or alcoholics to drink with. I also had a great fondness for fine wines, gins and whisky.

When I was thirty three, I met a great woman. She was intellectual, cultured, charismatic and a good pool player. She was also very beautiful. We fell in love, more or less at first sight. After two years, we married. The passion wore off and after seven years we divorced. My part in the failure of the marriage was not, I think, the drinking in itself. It was the fact that alcohol was much more important to me than she was. Alcohol was my true lover. I did not have much emotional space for any mere human.

It became clear to those close to me that I was an alcoholic. They told me this and provided excellent evidence. It meant nothing to me. Eventually, my doctor sent me to a counsellor who tried to teach me controlled drinking. After six months of therapy, I learned to control my drinking. Every waking hour that I spent not drinking, I spent planning those fifty units a week. The control didn't last long!

I began to drink in the mornings and throughout the day. I did not seek out sordid places. Instead I turned my nice apartment into one, as a more-or-less open house for the local street drunks and druggies. I enjoyed the company and liked the people. But it was chaos. The police were constantly called. I ceased to be popular with my neighbours. Of my fellow bohemians from that period, three are now dead (two ODs and one liver failure), and one, having landed on his head one time while drunk, has lost the ability to speak and lives in a care home.

While I was still clinging to a job, my psychiatrist sent me to rehab. There I was introduced to AA. Brought up as a devout atheist, and knowing science and philosophy, I knew I was never going to believe in any God. It was not a question of willingness to believe. My mind works in terms of evidence and argument. It doesn't do faith. The "God" talk in AA put me off. But I could see a lot of drunks getting sober. I found meetings difficult, boring, formulaic, and full of religion. I tried to listen to the similarities, not the differences, but I failed. I was too self-absorbed to listen to anything much, or to feel the emotional support in the rooms. And I did not relish the prospect of sobriety. I thought life would be dull and joyless at best.

After I left rehab I relapsed immediately. I went back in, came out, and relapsed immediately again. I lost my job. I ended up living a nightmare, terrified for my physical and mental health and my future, hardly able to feed myself, unable to do anything but drink. If I drank enough, I could experience brief periods of escape: a sort of serenity through anaesthesia. But also, when drunk enough, I would do dangerous things. Once I collapsed and my head collided with the corner of a large TV. I knew nothing of this until I woke up with a bloodied dent in my head and a TV on the floor. Another time, in a fury, I deliberately put my fist through a stained-glass window. I left a stream of blood on the floor as I staggered to my sofa and passed out.

I knew drink was destroying me. I was its slave. Without realising it, I took Steps One, Two and Three. That meant going back to rehab and for once doing everything that I was told (other than pray) without question or argument. My therapist gave me an atheist version of the Steps. I found an atheist sponsor. For Step Three, I elected a sort of advisory board: my sponsor, some people in AA, some outside. I turned all important decision-making over to them: I sought their advice and took it. This was a great experience for me: finally to stop running on self-will, to let go and go with the flow. I also learned to open my mind and my ears and listen at meetings. I have learned far more about myself from listening to other alcoholics than I did from many years of therapy. I like meetings now and I hear the similarities, not the differences. I know I am among people like me.

I did the Steps quickly and ended up in a decent psychological ("spiritual") place. But I had not listened or read well enough and I did not keep up the Step work, only going to two meetings a week and doing nothing else.

I declined very quickly. I feared financial insecurity. I would need a drink. I would deserve one. For three days I planned that drink. Not once did it cross my mind that there was any risk. It was as if half my mind had gone on holiday. I looked at my bank accounts, had the drink, then drank pure spirits non-stop for eleven days. A neighbour came and rescued me and got me a home detox. Two days into the detox, and feeling good, I lost the use of my legs for twelve hours. That scared me. A lot.

Then I had an idea! Work on the Steps every day. That worked like a miracle. I've had no troubling desire to drink since that moment. These have been the happiest three years of my life. I am mostly retired now, though I still pursue my research. I have returned to some activities of my youth: writing poetry, working with clay, going to concerts (mostly rock, mostly heavy metal, punk and hippy music). With my ears open and my attention directed outward, I enjoy music more than I ever did before.

And I work for AA in various administrative and public information roles. I enjoy that too, genuinely glad to be of service. I feel it is an honour and a privilege.

I am free of the discontent from which I suffered for fifty-odd years. I try to live in the real world now, rather than fantasy worlds of my own creation. The world is my higher power and I am content being who I really am, in it as it really is. Through meditation I can be at one with the flowers and I can find serenity without anaesthesia.

Since I don't believe in miracles, I turned my mind to studying how the Steps work. From my academic point of view, the answer is simple, evident on a psychological reading of the Big Book and the Twelve and Twelve (in my view, some of the finest psychological writing in existence), and largely vindicated by contemporary neuroscience. What causes relapse is emotional turbulence, which is caused by anger, resentment, fear, guilt, wounded pride, low self-esteem, envy, unsatisfied wants, existential angst and the like or by excessive elation. These cause a release of a specific hormone (corticotropin-releasing factor) that sends the dopamine system into overdrive, causing a strong desire to drink and at the same time impairing thought and memory. (That's my theory, anyway!).

Through inventory, sharing, making amends, meditation, helping others and trying to do the right thing, let go and leave the rest up to nature, I have learned how to calm my emotions, to accept others and feel accepted by them, to feel connected to the world and the sentient, feeling beings in it, to feel worthy of my place in the universe.

Emotional turbulence (the cause of stress and relapse) is caused by unmanaged, misdirected, over-active instincts. And what keeps instincts at bay are humility and spirituality, as I understand it: the opposite of self-will, self-seeking and self-absorption. As the result of the Steps, I have had a spiritual awakening.

12. God Problems

Betsy M.

My father got sober in AA in 1952. He drove two hours round trip to the nearest city to attend the only weekly meeting in his region. I was five, but I have no memories of my father as a drinker. He didn't try to frighten us kids away from alcohol, but he did tell us that AA was the place to go if we ever "got into trouble" with booze. As far as I knew, my father had never lied to me, so in 1984 I took his advice. I was 37, and I had been unsuccessfully trying to control my drinking. At my first meeting, I felt hopeful. I realized that I could get sober in AA. Though I saw no one at that meeting who seemed "like me", I identified with at least one thing each person said. After the meeting, a scary looking guy came up to me and said: "Just don't drink, even if your ass falls off". That I received his warning as sage advice certainly speaks to how ready I was for AA.

In the small town where I got sober, I ran into God problems almost immediately. My first roadblock was The Big Book. I couldn't stand it. It struck me as a self-help book for Christian men from my father's generation. I am a woman, a feminist and an atheist who came of age in the 1960s, not the 1940s. The Book was not written with me in mind, and no matter how hard I tried to twist the language to make it fit, it didn't.

The second roadblock was The Lord's Prayer. One of my regular meetings closed with that prayer. At first, I didn't recite the prayer, not because the words offended me, but because I don't believe them. A few well-meaning people urged me to "fake it 'til you make it". I didn't want to bring negative attention to myself, so I decided to conform. I felt in my gut that if I was going to keep coming to AA, which I absolutely had to do, I needed to avoid alienating myself from the people whose help I needed.

After my first anniversary, I got a sponsor. Like all the AA women I knew, her higher power was God. In fact, she had just converted to Catholicism. She was, fortunately, willing to allow me to work the Steps without trying to force me to define a higher power for myself. She told me not to worry, that she understood that "some of us take longer than others". By the time I got to my 5th Step, I was trying to be opened-minded. I thought maybe I should give the higher power thing a try. I had met a lot of people who seemed happily sober. And while I was grateful to be sober, I was certainly not happy during those first couple of years.

I began my exploration with a book of daily readings, consisting of an AA-related reflection, followed by a prayer. Although I tried to approach this sincerely, saying the prayer made me feel like a phony, so I gave it up. I also met with a professor of theology, a friend of a friend. She gave me interesting things to read, from many monotheistic traditions, and we met once a month to discuss them. I found many of the writers intelligent and persuasive. Still, I was not persuaded. By my third year, I decided I had given God an honest try, and I returned to my former belief (or nonbelief). I didn't share my decision with anyone because I didn't know anyone I thought would accept it. I remember I felt lonely about that. I had a family and a demanding job. Otherwise, I might have looked outside my town for some meetings with like-minded women.

By the time I'd been sober six years, I was going to only one meeting a week. I appreciated my sober life. I liked the person I had become, and I never had a desire to drink. I also hadn't changed my ways in AA. I was friendly with only a handful of people. I didn't go to retreats, or listen to tapes, or join in AA social events. After I completed the steps, I drifted away from my sponsor, and didn't look for another. Though I was respected in meetings as someone with solid sobriety and a good message, I was rarely asked to sponsor, perhaps because I wasn't an insider. Also, I didn't usually reach out to newcomers because I didn't feel I could be honest about my atheism. It's hard to guide someone through the Steps and avoid the God talk. I believed newcomers were better off if they could fit in. In 1994, when I was ten years sober, I was in a new relationship and began skipping my Sunday morning meeting. In a few months, I drifted away.

In 2004, after a decade away from AA, I returned. I had experienced a number of losses, and I thought meetings might chase away my despair. It worked. I soon felt better – more hopeful, more energetic. I was, however, disappointed to see that AA was still conservative. At that time, many newcomers were calling themselves "cross-addicted", and they were meeting resistance. Some of the members, mostly "old-timers", claimed that AA is for alcoholics only. Though the label "cross-addicted" was never banned, those who used it knew they were being tolerated more than accepted. I was twenty years sober, and I still didn't know another AA atheist.

In 2005, I moved to another small town in a nearby state. The town was politically progressive, so I assumed that would spill over into AA. Not so. If anything I found meetings to be even more structured with less opportunity for free discussion. Fortunately, I finally did meet a couple of fellow travelers, Thom and Dominick. We began to talk about the need for a meeting for agnostics and atheists. Thom researched agnostic AA meetings online and printed out some materials, including an alternative form of the Twelve Steps. We were good to go. We named our group "We Are Not Saints". We spread the word, at first, by announcing it at other meetings. Though we heard some grumbling and rumors of opposition, we had no trouble getting the meeting listed. Our group has been meeting for several years with a steady attendance of 10-15, many of whom are newcomers.

After 30 years, I can unequivocally say that I owe my sober self to AA. I doubt I would have made it through my first sober decade without going to meetings. I am cheering the current movement of freethinkers for challenging conservative AA. In 2014, my buddies, Thom and Dominick, attended the first AA convention for agnostics, atheists and freethinkers in Santa Monica. They returned beyond enthusiastic about the potential for this new movement.

If it succeeds, and AA begins to welcome and accept agnostics, atheists and freethinkers, countless suffering alcoholics who see AA as a religious organization will begin to lead sober lives, comfortable in the rooms of AA.

13. Another Apostate in Sobriety

Kit G.

Apostate: Noun, a person who renounces a religious or political belief or principle.

Looking back over my life I have always been part of culture or cult; my identity derived from the group philosophy whether family, nation, religion, sect, football team, or recovery affiliation. My problem has been a sense of self that depended on whatever group I was in, and being OK with it. Adopting and shedding labels has been a life-long process; some of it normative, some of it not.

The firstborn of five military brats to a Navy nurse and medic, the higher powers of my first 15 years were mom, dad, the U.S. Navy, and the deities of the Roman Catholic Church, in that order. From what I remember it was a relatively happy childhood.

Then the Sixties happened. Parental dysfunction, alcohol, sexuality, drugs, music, assassinations, the Vietnam War; world, social, and personal unrest all collided with my own self-centered fears to set me on a 28 year path of searching for a replacement of my childhood sense of ease, comfort and security. That searching included not only drugs and alcohol but a twelve year stint in a fringe evangelical Christian fundamentalist group and various other beliefs both, western, eastern, and new-age. Add to that a 31 year marriage having one child, the first 20 years of which were soothed by alcohol, and the last 10 of which were nothing more than what some call dry, untreated alcoholism.

Alcohol was always within reach. Grampa's home brew and wine as an altar boy were my first tastes of the heavenly elixirs. In high school I became a weekend blackout drinker all the while expected to be the devout Roman Catholic. Then I enlisted in the Navy due to my fears of being drafted and sent to Vietnam. Little did I realize that I had jumped from the frying pan into the fire, as they made me a medic. And medics, as you may not know, went with the Marines!

Fueled by my resentments about my parents' imminent divorce and destruction of my childhood security, mixed with my fears of an uncertain future, I used the cloak of the virtues of the anti-war movement to protest my unrighteous involvement in it. The Navy was not impressed. After a fellow friend and co-worker had been killed in action, I resorted to less desirable means to get myself removed from their employ. I was willing to go to any length to save myself, even a lifelong label of being a gay drug addict. The military didn't consider alcohol abuse or alcoholism a problem back then, at least not openly, so I couldn't have used that even if I had been aware of it, even though I had rolled my car in another drunken blackout.

Not long after my undesirable discharge and more excessive use of alcohol and any kind of drugs I could get my hands on, I got religion again. It was 1970 and Jesus People were everywhere; militant, and strange ones at that. I joined the Children of God and became intoxicated, as John Bradshaw described in Healing the Shame that Binds You, on righteousness. This is where I met my late wife and made feeble attempts at responsibility and relationship, all the while dependent on my addictive nature for relief or escape when times got tough.

Our son was born in '82 and more responsibility meant the need for more relief and reward, and that meant more drinking. By 1992 I figured my alcohol use might be the cause of my then marital, financial, and mental distress. Actually, my drinking was becoming more problematic than my other stressors. Facing bankruptcy, divorce and unemployment, I went to my first AA meeting with a sincere desire to stop drinking and it worked. That desire, combined with the fellowship and comradery, displaced my need to drink. I got what I came for and stopped going to meetings after two months but read the books for the next ten years as my wife and life became more unmanageable without alcohol. I adopted lots of other issues to cope; mostly materialism, work-a-holism, affairs of the actual or emotional variety, smoking, and occasional pill popping.

I became extremely depressed, or as a friend said, "just depressing". I didn't know it at the time but that ten year span was my first and longest experience as a "dry drunk", and I fully experienced the emotional lows that can be reached without self-medication. My family wished I'd return to drinking, when I'd seemed happier.

After reading tons of self-help, relationship, psychology, and new-age books, I went to a therapist on my own. It helped. Then my wife died and our only son began his tear into his own searching and left. Sober and alone for the first time in my life, I met a woman member of AA and went to a meeting on a date. I don't know who was more desperate. After ten years without a meeting I felt at home again.

I got a sponsor, did the steps Joe and Charlie style (an old fundamental by the book way), got into service, some sponsoring, AA conventions, and daily meetings; all the while being frustrated with the "god talk" and feeling agnostic but wanting to fit in and not make waves. I had always felt this conflict from the beginning in AA but was willing and desperate enough to sit with it, translate it, or ignore it in order not to drink and be part of the fellowship. I was letting AA become another cult to me.

Everyone was saying that step work was integral to my inner happiness and usefulness, so I listened to hundreds of speakers and Big Book thumper's recordings and step studies. I wanted sobriety but I also wanted to sound good and be liked, as well as grow. After about five years sober I discovered Edward Bear's series of books, starting with The Dark Night of Recovery, which had just the right amount of irreverence and free-thinking for me at the time. I closed many a meeting with, "Great Pumpkin, grant me the serenity..." Looking back, this is where conference "unapproved" literature began enhancing my emotional sobriety and free-thinking.

While working the steps with other members, I began to put the steps and attendant prayers into my own words for myself as best I could and felt much happier about it. I found that the language of religion or the Big Book was insufficient to communicate the language of my heart. I think what turned the key for me was the line in the Big Book that says, "The wording was, of course, quite optional so long as we express the idea, voicing it without reservation". It was liberating to take that to heart!

How could I talk about or pray to a god I honestly did not believe existed anymore? So, I have discarded the mythological and gone for the tangible. The group itself, its collective consciousness, the idea that "the whole is greater than the sum of its parts", the principles of the "we" factor, and the expansion of that idea to include not only AA but all of humanity, are all powers greater than me. Also, the idea expressed in Appendix II about an "unsuspected inner resource" that we are all born with has marked my path and that gods are metaphors for human characteristics and principles, not the principles themselves.

By 2011 I had read *Waiting: a Nonbelievers Higher Power* by Marya Hornbacher, and realized I was agnostic and still felt out of step and distanced by all the god talk and prayers in the fellowship. I didn't realize I was finding my own voice and language. I became OK with not having to gravitate towards the belief in anyone else's mythology as I feel I am expected to do in the chapter "We Agnostics" in the Big Book. I feel that as an agnostic, atheist, or realist member of AA, I'm finally being part of a whole that is inclusive. I am being honest with myself and tolerant of others and sense a profound equilibrium with that. The need for a few drinks that others take with impunity is no longer necessary to feel this way. The principles of Alcoholics Anonymous don't care what I do or don't believe because they are not allied with any faith, sect or denomination, although you wouldn't know it at most meetings.

When I discovered *Beyond Belief* by Joe C. and AA Agnostica in January of 2014, I realized I was also an atheist at least to a degree. My apostasy has grown just as my former beliefs did, and of course, are being replaced by new beliefs which I'm sure will also change. Coming to believe is often preceded by coming to not believe. Some old ideas just don't work anymore. I acknowledged a growing sense of indignation and anger, a desire to stand up for what I felt, especially after reading about the prejudices that were occurring elsewhere regarding delisting of agnostic and atheist meetings by "governing" AA intergroups.

At this point I remember exploring many books on atheism and feeling a sense of loss, grief, and uncertainty. Fear of what it would be like to be without a god, capital G or not. Fear of what others would think and say. It was frightening and still is at times but it has now become more challenging to explore what I really think and feel is most meaningful in each moment. I had allowed the beliefs of others to dominate my thinking for so long I felt as though my own thinking muscles had become atrophied, crippled, and dependent on the approval of others.

Eleanor Roosevelt once said, "When you adopt the standards and values of someone else... you surrender your own integrity [and] become, to the extent of your surrender, less of a human being". The challenge is keeping my own integrity while making said values and standards my own. This is the trial and error process of being a human being and what Ernie Kurtz called the "spirituality of imperfection".

In June of 2014 after six months of stewing in that discomfort, I and a few others started our own open group of Alcoholics Anonymous for Atheists, Agnostics and All others. (Yes, that's 5 A's.) I did it for me and because of the several alcoholics who have died in my community in recent years. They were atheist, agnostic, or terribly oppressed and self-loathing Christians. I want others who feel as I to have a place to come and share their innermost selves, including and especially their doubts, without shame or fear of being rejected or coerced into believing in somebody else's traditional outlooks whether religious or atheistic.

What it's like now? Now I want to and have to explore all of my thinking, instincts, and motives with the freedom, challenge and responsibility that I find in the principles of the steps and elsewhere, based on my own understanding and wording which is continually evolving to meet current needs and feelings. Confirmation bias is hopefully kept in check by steps five and ten's suggestions to check my views with others.

> Now I become myself. It's taken
> Time, many years and places;
> I have been dissolved and shaken,
> Worn other people's faces

So begins a poem by May Sarton. Those words for me represent the ease and comfort as well as depth and weight I have so long sought and continue to yearn for. I have grown tired of wearing other peoples' faces. I want to know myself as well as others. Does identity formation ever stop? I don't think so. As I have heard in the rooms, "I have a yearning disability". Only it's not a disability, it's just human. It's a normal human instinct, a thirst. To desire connection, food, shelter, companionship, and security is the root of human development on one hand and the root of addiction on the other; normal instincts versus instincts gone wild.

Emotional sobriety is my current and continuing frontier. It has to be. These squirrelly things called feelings are in a confluence with my thinking and behavior more than anything else. They seem to be intimately attached to those instincts mentioned above. They are acutely reactionary and defensive and seem to transport me out of the moment more often than not. Flights of fantasy into the future whether fearful or pleasurable, or regrets and remorse over the past; both keep my emotional sobriety date at about five seconds ago.

But that's OK. Length of sobriety of any kind is, as I have heard, a bankrupt currency by itself. Depth and breadth of sobriety is what I'm interested in. I have helped to create a fellowship around me that is truly "roomy, all inclusive; never exclusive or forbidding".

My name is Kit G. and I have been un-continuously sober for 66 years, and today is the first day of the rest of my sobriety.

14. My Diluted Emotions

Deirdre S.

I drank for twenty years. Too many times I drank past my tolerance level and woke up shivering on some bathroom floor. When I picked up my first beer of the night, I rarely knew how or where I'd end up. In the mornings, I often felt like someone had slipped me poison. Of course that mysterious "someone" was me.

My last and final drunk wasn't my last and final drink. After a terrible night, wasted, stumbling, and trying to find my way home only five short blocks from my apartment, I knew I couldn't go one more round with alcohol. Stopping completely seemed too final. I decided that I needed to lay off for a few months. I drank a couple of beers here and there while I contemplated the right time to begin my R and R (resisting and rehydration). Finally an acquaintance suggested acupuncture. Initially this worked; I went ten days without a drink, for me a long interval. But I found, underneath all the drinking, I had a lot of un-dealt-with emotions I'd been diluting.

A sober friend urged me to go to an AA meeting. During the twenty years that I'd been drinking I had come in contact with the 12 Steps of Alcoholics Anonymous. Each time I read them the word God loomed high. I've been an atheist since I was twelve. I never had the need or desire to have a divine being in my life. When I said to my sober friend that I couldn't go to AA she said that she was also an atheist, but found what she needed to stay sober were meetings and the fellowship.

At my first meeting I stayed quiet. During a discussion about Step One a big Irish guy, former bartender, said that the step had nothing to do with God. He boiled down the program to: Don't drink; Go to meetings; and Help another alcoholic. Keep it simple he said. Relief swept over me. I could take what I heard in meetings, identify with the stories, and stay sober.

However, I still needed more to maintain long-term sobriety. I needed the fellowship and the experience, strength, and hope of others. I needed to find a meeting where I could let those emotions I'd been drowning come to the surface.

About six months into my sobriety, I found a meeting that catered to agnostics, atheists, and freethinkers as well as anyone else who needed a giant dose of AA. At that meeting I met people who had decades of sobriety, but never prayed a day in their lives. I met people who had tried all the suggestions of well-meaning AAs, but still found that praying did not feel like rigorous honesty – no matter how hard they tried. When they surrendered to the idea that they couldn't drink safely, they accepted their powerlessness over alcohol. These sober people were members of AA, no better or worse than people who believed in God.

Everyone, it seems, had their own definition of spirituality and that confused me. But after I stopped the intake of the depressant alcohol, I felt better. I got my "joy of life" back. That's as close as I come to having a spiritual experience and I was thrilled to discover that my booze-induced cloud of lousy feelings vanished. Even the streets of New York City looked brighter. My grumpy attitude transformed and my co-workers saw the difference in the clearness of my eyes.

I look to my fellows every time I get an urge to drink. If I find myself in a situation where I can't call one of them for support, I imagine their healthy sober faces. I learned that I could leave parties and other social situations if I felt uncomfortable about the drinking. I shared lots of coffee with sober people. Slowly they became my friends. I found a sponsor and did the steps with her. Some parts of AA literature I liked, other parts I couldn't identify with. But I've both found what I needed for long-term sobriety in meetings and fellowship.

I've been sober for eighteen years now. I'm happy with the profound changes I've made. My life is bigger than I ever imagined. I'm glad the hand of AA was there for me. I do service so that AA will be there for others when they decide it's time to quit hurting themselves. I'm grateful that I found a home meeting where people have accepted me as I am, encouraged me to grow, and demanded that I remain true to my better self.

15. A New Man

David B.

Coming to: What happened? Where am I? Who am I? Most alcoholics are familiar with this feeling: an abyss of loss and then a desperate search for the events that led to this point. Sometimes there's nothing, sometimes there's a flash – of momentarily seeing, understanding something, but that disappears in a flash, too. And then sometimes – if you're as determined as I've always been – you will chase the flash that might, eventually, lead you to your awakening, a new coming to; a reality where you can finally function without having to compromise your true self.

* * *

In December of 2004, I came to with several emergency technicians around me; there was noise: words, words, words... Maybe words? People yelling, at me, to me: trying to engage me in a conversation – asking me if I could hear them, if I knew where I was. My wife, there too, pleading with me to come out of it, come to.

Come to what? I felt confused.

What date, where was I, did I know what happened? The questions kept on, or maybe they were asked once and my brain was only getting to them now, after playing them on the loop. Words.

So I said some words back, answered some questions. I tried.

My body wasn't cooperating either – it was sore; it was a body beat up from contracting, seizing, twitching. My tongue screamed with pain: I bit it, repeatedly, just moments ago.

A grand mal seizure.

Finally, there was clarity in the chaos – words coming together, aligning with their meaning. My wife's eyes looking at me with relief. Vicki. I was coming to. Back to reality. Vicki could see that I would live.

And in four months, thanks to the seizure, I would question this life that I was coming to.

I lost my driver's license. There were medical tests: Why did I have the seizure? I told the doctors about painkillers and drinking too much but that wasn't it – although after my confession, I was prescribed Topamax, which creates monster hangovers. My anxiety was monstrous too. There were more medical tests. The doctors said I was possibly epileptic. They wanted to know where the seizure came from. It wasn't the first one and as months went on, there was pressure to learn my medical history.

What complicated things was the fact that I was adopted. I had to find out more: it seemed my life depended on it.

And here's what I found: Miss Bender, 56 years old, died in 1996 of alcoholism. My biological mother. My DNA, my medical history. (Me: "Baby Boy Bender" on the birth certificate – that last name, a grand irony or what?)

I couldn't deal with it, with my genetics – like me drowning in Jack Daniels, that was yet another truth I didn't want a part of. So I did what every addict does when confronted with reality: I put that information in a box – figuratively, literally – and the progression of my alcoholism went off the charts.

* * *

Nine-plus months later, picture this: a grown man bawling his eyes out in front of a room full of strangers.

My name is, I say – but everything – like these people, this room – remains unfamiliar for a moment. Even my name and who I am. And whatever happened in the past 24 hours is a blur of one tormented, interrupted sleep; flashbacks of my son and my wife bringing me clothes, other things… a fog of events, feelings of humiliation, too, as my body detoxed.

Then I was off to the treatment center; there was a five minutes-long assessment; more confusion – Who am I? Why am I here? – and I was thrown into this room. An AA meeting.

And now, in this room, bawling; all eyes on me – compassionate eyes, encouraging eyes of people who understand why I'm bawling -I finally choke it out: My name is David and I'm an alcoholic.

Instantly, I feel an immense relief: I know who I am. Only for a flash at this point, but it's the first time I recognize something concrete about myself.

There's shame too – for now, only the leftover shame any alcoholic feels; the shame that haunts and often makes sobriety seem like the worst idea ever because you'll have to face it, the shame. But in this moment, saying the words, admitting who I am, the relief is bigger than the shame; the desire to stop drinking is genuine. It trumps the shame. The shame will come back – it will haunt me for years – but right now even the shame is only a shadow; it waits for me to finish coming to in this room full of strangers. They are bearing witness to a man dying and becoming a new man right before their eyes – the eyes who already know everything without knowing anything specific about me. What they know – everything – is that I am coming back to reality.

* * *

Every day, I am a new man. This has been a theme in my life. As a sober alcoholic, being a new man every day helps me keep in touch with the world around me: I must always be aware of my perception and how close it is to reality. The closer the better.

I am close today.

Wait. Let me check: yes, I am still here. Still sober.

Today, my perception is aligned with my reality.

* * *

You see, addicts have a problem with perception – this is not because we're stupid; we're just used to life that is based on manipulation, double-think, secrets – any thing to confirm our delusions. We're used to not wanting to see things for how they are – we especially avoid the truth of our addiction. And even when we see it, our addiction, we are helpless against it: just because you know something is very wrong, it doesn't mean you know how to treat it.

When we drink or use, we try to mold the world around us to suit the addiction – for example, I've spent years in my basement office, drinking and watching television. One show, Intervention, sticks in mind – the ridiculousness of it: me, an addict, watching other addicts. Me watching addicts drink themselves to death while drinking myself to death. It's not that I thought that that was the right thing to do – sitting there and making myself die, slowly – it's just that I did it because it suited me at the time. My perception wasn't aligned with my reality. But it allowed me to avoid everything that was happening outside of the basement. Like the world that was happening upstairs, the real world.

Upstairs, outside the basement, there was my daughter and son, and my wife.

Upstairs, there I was: a successful businessman.

Upstairs, there I was: a social guy with an ability to draw people. There was a beautiful lake and a lifestyle that was fun and full of adventure.

But then look back in to the basement: there I was, too, drinking. Alone. There I was: a man who self-imprisoned with all kinds of alcohol and a cooler full of ice, no food, in the same basement; a three-day-long bender. (Coming to with my face planted in my keyboard: Where am I? Did anyone see me like this?

My son did. He saw me passed out and he called my wife. I found out later he thought I was dead; my wife told him to spend the night at a friend's place.)

But I made it all work – no, it didn't work at all.

It was my perception that deceived me – my perception was warped; it allowed all of that to co-exist, however dysfunctional.

There was something else there the whole time: that box with a secret. The box where I knew something about myself but wasn't sure how to deal with. My mother, how she died, how she… relinquished me. Another twist in this tale of who I was or wasn't.

* * *

The definition of perception is three things: "The way you think about or understand someone or something; the ability to understand or notice something easily; the way that you notice or understand something using one of your senses." Was I doomed? Perhaps. Because how could I ever have the right perception of the guy I was if, at the age of 44, after the seizure, I learned I was somebody else entirely?

The facts: my biological mother died of alcoholism. I drank constantly.

There was no coming out of darkness without facing it – all of it – properly. But you can't face anything when you can't think or understand, or even use your senses. When your perception is a deformity.

And even today, sober, that guy is a part of me, or rather that story is a part of me, like my mysterious DNA – and this is why I check in with reality all the time. This is why I question my perception. I must. I am not living in a delusion of addiction any more but it's easy to slip into it.

For an alcoholic, it takes a second – or not even a second, a millisecond – to lose the reality of addiction. Since 2005, I haven't had a relapse but I've heard and read about them enough to be aware of them.

For now, I'm David and I'm an alcoholic. And I just have to remember that I am that man, a new man. Every day.

* * *

I don't just mean this metaphorically since as an adoptee and an alcoholic, I come by my newness honestly. I've led the kind of split existence that can only be dealt with by ignoring it, numbing what I knew, and didn't know. I refer to myself as a relinquishee – rejected by his birth parents but also having to adapt to the reality of my adopted family. Because of this, I've always had problems with attachment and reaching out to people... my sense of rejection shadowed my whole life. So I drank over that too. Alcohol silenced the war that was going on in my head – me against myself; the adoptee versus the adopted.

* * *

Sobriety was the number-one place where I felt at home. After that first meeting, I sat in dozens of group sessions at the rehab facility, still full of skepticism, fear, confusion. The shame was sneaking its way back, but for now I immersed myself in my recovery. In the sessions, I watched the people I dubbed COINS: Commuity of Individuals Needing Support – people who needed the same support I did. They were like coins because there were so many of them: they came from NA, AA, Marijuana Anonymous... There were also volunteers and professionals who talked about relapse prevention strategies, disease of addiction – finally, spirituality. I didn't always understand what was being taught but I was determined: I had to adapt to survive. And I knew two things; One: If these people are wrong I will never trust anyone ever, again, and Two: If they're wrong, I'm dead.

I secured a mentor, a sponsor who right after I graduated from rehab said, You're not going home to sleep in your own bed – you are going to an AA meeting. And that's where I went.

* * *

It was where I stayed: 450 meetings in the first 365 days of my sobriety. I read every bit of AA-approved literature I could put my hands on; then I read some things mentioned in the Big Book such as The Varieties of Religious Experiences by William James.

I sold my house on the lake to change my former lifestyle – full of drinking buddies, well-meaning neighbors who greeted me from rehab with a welcome basket, a 1.75 liter bottle of Jack Daniels perched on top – and I attended conferences, readings... I went back to the same rehab facility six months into sobriety to passion-ately talk about my new life.

And I lived happily ever after.

* * *

No I didn't. I tried. Very hard. What was standing in my way was Shame, again. And now I was finding it in the rooms of AA!

I kept finding it because I was missing something – a crucial thing, specifically god. I kept hearing, Let go and let God. I was told I was too self-centered; I wasn't able to turn my life over to my (?) Higher Power; I had to set aside my pride and my ego; make room for this god who kept evading me.

God. Where was she?

I looked for her, for god, everywhere as the shame of not being able to find her, of not fitting in, again, was getting bigger and bigger. I tried to immerse myself, to come to a spiritual experience that included god.

So I read about god. I talked about god to rabbis and pastors, and during lunches, I sat in a beautiful St. Andrew's church near my workplace, waiting for god to appear. I prayed day and night… but to what?

I suppose I was praying to lure her out, make her appear like a genie from a bottle. And speaking of bottles – my fear was that I was going to go back to it, the bottle, if I didn't find this god.

This went on for eight, grueling, shame-filled years.

Sit back. Relax. God will get in touch with you. God exists: after all, God graced you with sobriety.

It made no sense to me. I was getting hopeless.

My perception was getting blurred.

* * *

Except there was hope. There was a new coming to.

I had a specific tool and it was the same one as always: immersing myself in something and this time it was going on a quest but a completely opposite one of the one I had been on. Because, I thought, surely, there are others like me out there? Just like there were other relinquishees in the world, there must be others in the program who also couldn't make sense out of the god part.

There were. Lots of them.

First in books:

> Appendix II in *Alcoholics Anonymous*
>
> *Beyond Belief: Agnostic Musings for 12 Step Life*
>
> *The Little Book: A Collection of Alternative 12 Steps*
>
> *Don't' Tell: Stories and Essays by Agnostics and Atheists in AA*
>
> *An Atheist's Unofficial Guide to AA – For Newcomers*
>
> *Waiting: A Nonbeliever's Higher Power*
>
> *The Five Keys: 12 Step Recovery Without A God*

Then in on-line chat rooms and blogs, and so I immersed myself yet again, this time into a like-minded community within the program that made me come to originally.

* * *

Essentially, the story of my life are genetic clues, a series of coming-tos, adapting to a recovery program where I didn't quite fit in and then, finally, coming to my senses, my feelings and my values.

I realized I needed to conduct myself in alliance with who I truly was instead of adapting and using all of my energy – the energy that was needed in my life outside of recovery, my family, my career – to try to fit in. This new, agnostic reality was perfectly aligned with mine – this reality gave me permission to finally find my true place in the world.

It was in the rooms of agnostic AA where I became the new man that I am now – a man who's a whole bunch of parts and contradictions but who is also whole, most true to himself and his reality.

Coming to: a new man.

16. Take Three Degrees. Add Alcohol.

Martine R.

The decision to stop drinking alcohol, once and for all, is one I shall never regret. I will soon celebrate 13 years of sobriety, after three decades of active alcoholism. Because I am now a different, better person, my life is a different, better life. It is that simple. And yet, the journey to that simple and logical decision was long and hard and painful.

I was born and raised in France in a well-to-do family which included ancestors in the Bordeaux wine business. Being able to appreciate good wine was an indispensable part of good breeding. I never in those days associated wine with alcoholism. In fact, although wine was always served at meals, I do not remember ever wanting to drink it in large amounts.

My teen years were not happy. I was molested by my father. He was well-educated, respected and successful. In our social class, girls were expected to be proper young ladies, so they could marry respectable men. I therefore lived in an irreconcilable situation, where the very person who was supposed to raise me properly was in fact an aggressor.

When I was about 16, I drank whiskey at a party, and become drunk and sick. However, I felt grown-up and sophisticated. After that first whiskey-induced drunkenness, I loved drinking, for many reasons. First, when I got tipsy, my confusion and shame would abate for a while. Second, I was told that many of the great poets and artists were heavy drinkers, so I felt that creativity and originality went hand-in-hand with alcohol. Also, what was happening in secret at home gave me great disgust for the traditional image of womanhood all were trying to mold me into. I was supposed to be well-bred and proper? Oh no! I would drink and smoke and curse a blue streak, which was my way to rebel... I was doing very well at school and wanted more for myself than just finding a good husband.

One summer when I was 18, my favorite aunt took me to the United States for summer vacation. There I happened to meet a boy my age and we fell in love. He came to France the next summer and as he was about to return to the States, we found out

I was pregnant. There was an uproar and much disapproval in both families, of course. I went to the US, we were quickly married. We lived at first with my husband's parents. Our daughter was born there, at about the time her father was graduating from college. Then he went to Medical school for four years.

We had almost no money. Buying alcohol of any kind, even cheap wine, was impossible. I took whatever small jobs I could find, I was a waitress, a nanny, and eventually I taught French in a small private school.

After my husband graduated from Medical school we moved to California where he did his internship and residency. Our financial situation was improving a little; I was also able to get a scholarship for a Master's degree in French. I wanted to have better credentials to get better teaching jobs. We had a second child. Then after having obtained my Master's, I was offered another scholarship to do a Ph.D. There was a lot of work and a lot of juggling between work and child care.

Every once in a while I could buy a bottle of wine to drink with meals. I felt civilized again. Every once in a while, I did get drunk. I was not worried about it. I felt it was a necessary outlet, it hurt no one, it was all in fun. And it was only wine, which, as everyone knows, is good for you…

The major event of those years was my husband being drafted and having to go to Vietnam for a year. I remember that year almost as if in a dream. I was completely petrified that my husband might be hurt or killed. I lived in terror of not being a good enough mother to protect the children while I was alone with them. Somehow we all survived. I probably drank a little during that year, but not much. I did not dare. Obviously, I was then at a stage where I still had some control.

Our next move after that year in Vietnam was back to the East Coast, to Baltimore, where my husband got his first real job teaching and practicing in a hospital. I found a teaching job at a nearby university. We bought a house and put the kids in good schools. We met a lot of nice people in our new neighborhood and we began to have a busy social life.

I was too busy to take much time to reflect and wonder about my life. What I considered quiet time, was to sit down with a glass of wine, I never ever questioned whether I was perhaps drinking too much. I had several episodes of getting drunk at parties but thought nothing of it.

Any reproach from my husband or snide remark from a friend I would dismiss, because they had no idea what I had gone through, no idea that drinking was an absolute necessity. I felt that without it, I would go mad. Wine was holding me together.

There was love and many other good things in my life. Our daughter got accepted at a prestigious college, the same one her father had been to, when she was just 16. Our son was doing well in a good school. He ended up going to the very same college. As far as I knew, I must be a good mother, since my kids were doing so well.

Despite all these appearances of success and happiness, I was feeling restless. I decided to go to Law School. I managed to pass all courses despite a lot of drinking. After graduation I got a good job as an associate in a small but well-connected firm. I was not a great success there. I had started drinking at lunch time, running home from the office to have some lunch and some wine. I went to bed early instead of working long hours and it had been noticed. Already, my drinking "a little too much" was no longer a secret. When I said we were moving, no one said they were sorry about it.

We moved again because my husband now took a position in Massachusetts. During the next fifteen years, I lost almost all control over my drinking. The children were no longer at home. My husband was busier than ever at the hospital. At first I got a job at a prestigious law firm, the best-known in that area. Then I left them when it became obvious they did not really "appreciate" me. I went to another firm, who thought, erroneously, that they were "snatching" me away. Little did they know that the prestigious firm was very happy to get rid of me. After a few years in that second law firm, I left again and ended up practicing law by myself.

As I look back on these 15 years, from where I am now, I see clearly the disaster that was unfolding, which I could not see at the time. There was a repeated pattern: First, I would impress people with my credentials (three graduate degrees, imagine that!). Then I would start surprising them by how little actual work I was doing and by not being at all a team player. There were a few times where I accomplished something, in or out of court, which was brilliant. But one does not build a career and gain a good reputation by just a few strokes of brilliance.

What was happening is that I had become a full-fledged alcoholic; I was moody, unpredictable and untrustworthy. I have no good memories from these years. At some point, I realized that I was drinking much too much. I decided I would reduce the amount I was drinking.

At this point of my story, my narrative becomes totally predictable, because I went through all the moves every desperate alcoholic goes through: drinking only after a certain time of the day; drinking only certain days of the week; stopping completely for a time, then starting again (because I was surely cured after stopping for three months!)

Nothing worked and my life was miserable. I did not want to live any more. I no longer had much of a family life or social life. I had no hope; I saw no light at the end of the tunnel.

And then my husband announced we were moving again, to a town near New York. I welcomed the move. It meant an end to my law career unless I could get admitted to the New York bar, but I did not care. I announced to everyone that I was going to practice law in New York State, but not immediately. First, I was going to take a sabbatical.

My sabbatical consisted, of course, in drinking more and more for about 18 months. I did not look for a new job. I did not try to make friends with anyone. I just drank. I was desperate, even suicidal. I kept telling myself "today is the last day drinking, I cannot go on like that". I wanted to stop drinking more than I had ever wanted anything, but I could not.

One day, about thirteen years ago, I was picking up our son at the railroad station to drive him somewhere. Once he had gotten in the car, he looked at me and said: "Mom, you look tired". "Tired" was the word he had always used when he saw that I was drunk. And he was right: While still able to drive, I had been having already a few glasses of wine and it was not even noon.

I had been caught being drunk many times before. This time, however, for some reason, it felt like the end of my world. I was so ashamed I almost collapsed. I did bring my son to his destination and returned home. Then I called AA.

I had heard about AA many times. As a lawyer, I sometimes took care of clients who had got into some scrapes because of drunkenness. When passing sentence or decreeing probation, the Court would usually demand that they attend AA meetings. Once, I had even gone to an AA meeting. There, I discovered that in order to become sober one must not drink AT ALL. I was horrified. That would not do for me. I needed my wine!

When I called AA that day in February thirteen years ago, a man told me he would meet me the next day at a meeting not far from my house. I went to that meeting. He greeted me and spoke to me kindly. It was February 22nd and the beginning of my new life.

I could not bear to say in public those words "I am an alcoholic". I started sobbing every time I tried. But I eventually managed to say it. By now, I have said these words thousands of time, and I know they are true.

All these years of struggle trying to stop drinking on my own ended with that first meeting. The obsession to drink was lifted. Something in me changed irrevocably when I heard one person after another person just like me, as sick as I was. The relief was enormous. I was not unique after all, not bad and shameful in a unique way as I had thought.

Then, I heard people tell about how much time sober they had. One woman had 25 years! Her husband had just died, she was obviously grieving, BUT SHE WAS STILL SOBER. When I realized that, I felt a surge of hope… a sensation I had not felt for so long. I, too, could become sober, it was possible! (That woman became my sponsor. She has helped me immensely by her gentle counsel, as has, by mere example, the man who introduced me to that meeting.)

It did not bother me much, at first, that the meeting often ended with the Lord's Prayer. I did wonder, though, about using a Christian prayer to close the meeting, in a country with so many different religions. As I attended more and more meetings, I began to be concerned about the very religious attitude of many AA members, especially when leaders of meeting aggressively declared that, in order to be sober, one had to "let God into one's life".

I happen to be an agnostic. While I respect the right of everyone to his or her own philosophy, I was disappointed that AA did not make itself more inclusive. That did not deter me from coming to meetings. I just resigned myself to hearing a lot of "God talk" and to keep my own counsel.

Then one day when I was about three years sober, as I was glancing at a list of AA meetings in Chicago, I saw the word "agnostic"; I was thrilled! I had never heard of agnostic AA meetings. I made inquiries and soon got a list of such meetings in New York City.

When I went to my first agnostic meeting, I felt some of the relief and hope I had experienced at my first meeting. This time it was the relief of being able to express myself freely. Basically, I felt fully included, which I had begun to despair of in regular meetings.

Now I can truly say that my sober life is more authentic and joyous and free than my drinking life. Those years of hiding the extent of my drinking are over. I no longer have to engage in constant damage control to hide all the failures and mishaps caused by drunkenness.

I did not return to the practice of law, but I found other uses for my new free time in sobriety, including doing service for AA and volunteering for a political cause I am passionate about. I now feel that my life is useful, not a total waste as before.

One does not escape entirely the "wreckage of the past". I did not get a blank pass for my past behavior. I have a difficult relationship with my grown children. I know they feel hurt by so many things I did or failed to do, and by my becoming sober so late in my life. They grew up with an active alcoholic, nothing can change that.

From Day One in AA, I felt hope. That has not stopped. I still have hope that somehow, by dint of dealing calmly and courageously with the after-effects of the past, I will be able to help others as others have helped me. I know this is not the end of the story.

17. My Path in AA

life j.

The path was not easy for this agnostic in AA.

I was an atheist when I got sober, as arrogant as most people with staunchly held beliefs. Sober, I have still never felt the presence of a god, but I have come to be open-minded, to accept that if other people think there is one, that's fine and none of my business, so long as they don't try to make me believe there is. But for a long time well meaning old-timers did, and of course I tried to believe them. I wanted to work this program right. Took more than ten years before they quit pestering me, and another ten before I could speak my mind freely about it.

The chapter "We Agnostics" in the Big Book at least acknowledged that there were people like me, but then it forged right ahead with arguing for the existence of god, and the assumption that surely sooner or later I would find god too. It was only a matter of staying sober a little longer and coming to my senses.

And I read the Big Book and even Came to Believe, but I never did.

I found a humanist meeting which I attended, and later I found another meeting where there was no "Lord's Prayer" at the end. It always offended me to have this piece of Christianity imposed upon me. The closing prayer was the one time during an AA meeting where I would feel truly alone, unless I spotted someone else in the circle with their lips sealed. Then we'd smile at each other and not feel so alone any more.

* * *

So I'm going to write about how I stayed sober without a higher power, and developed a spirituality which helped.

When a person comes into AA with even some inclination toward accepting a Christian-like god, there is already a well laid out program for them. Most of our literature is focused on this god, even with the caveat "as we understood him," but when the God concept remains completely foreign to us, we have to develop a spirituality all on our own. The kind of help that I could accept was scant and far between in the beginning. Finding a sponsor who wouldn't harass me about finding a higher power was real difficult.

One of the reasons that I don't like the higher power concept, and that the religious people are so insistent on it, is that it creates a continuum intended to sneak god in the back door. I can let the group be my higher power they say, but the idea is they aren't really content with that. Sooner or later they expect me to find the real god who isn't just any higher power, but the one and only.

I could have the group as my higher power, but why? True, I depend on the group to help me stay sober and grow, and with the help of the group I can do things I likely could not do on my own, but why does that have to make it a higher power?

We all accept the saying that two heads think better than one. So does that mean that the two heads together now become a higher power to the individual heads? Why is it not just two heads thinking together?

Or, like an AA friend of mine says, try lifting a heavy sack alone. It can be tough. Now try two of you together, it gets easier, now try four, of course it gets still easier, and the four of us together can lift something much heavier than one person can all alone. Where exactly does the higher power concept become needed to explain this? This is all the group does, lifts a burden together. We are doing together what we could never do alone. I simply see it as a level field, and no higher power is needed to explain how this program works.

The group is not my higher power, nothing is my higher power, and just because I don't have a higher power, does not mean that I am playing god, and just because I figure that there is no god in charge, does not mean that I am, or think I am, or that I am trying to be god.

Maybe this "playing god" was a problem for the high powered Type A professionals and businessmen who started this program, but my problem was fear, not a big ego. If it sometimes looked that way, maybe it was because of fear of losing territory, fear of losing respect, or love or money or whatever, sometimes fear of not getting what I wanted. I had two ways of dealing with it: Try to control the situation, or drink my feeling of failure away when it was obvious I couldn't control it.

So now sober, I couldn't stop trying to play god like they told me to because I never had to begin with. I had only done whatever it would take in the moment to not feel whatever I was about to feel, usually fear, and a poor choice which would take that bad feeling away right now was better than a good choice which would have solved the problem in five minutes.

Of course when I was drinking I was arrogant, self-centered, and self-serving, and it caused me all sorts of trouble. But is it not possible to find a way out of self-centeredness and self will without putting it in relation to the will of a god? Either it is my will, or god's will, they say, but where does god really fit into this? Can I not simply stop imposing my selfishness on the world with the help of other recovering alcoholics? With careful consideration of what sort of results self-centeredness got me, and compared to what sort of results a courteous, considerate, helpful manner of living gets me? Why is a god needed to explain that one works well, and the other doesn't? Isn't simple, common sense enough?

* * *

Eventually I came to a place of some humility. And here we need to talk about surrender.

This can be a hard concept to swallow at first, because we suspect that probably it again means surrender to a "higher power," or even a god. But is not surrender possible even without it being "to" anything? All it means is to say, "OK, I give up being selfish, self centered and self serving. I become teachable, service minded, and as generous and kind as I am able to be without opening myself to being deliberately taken advantage of by anybody." Isn't that enough? Why do I have to offer myself to a "thee"? I am offering myself to my fellow alcoholic, and my fellow man at large. AA is about one alcoholic talking with another, not about talking with god.

Surrender requires acceptance. And acceptance is not required because "nothing absolutely nothing happens in god's world by mistake," but rather because without first accepting myself as I am, I have no honest self appraisal on which I can base change. I wasn't playing god, I was just hard-headed. God or no god, acceptance is just to gain peace, to have a starting point from which to move forward.

* * *

I have learned that I don't need to have answers to all the world's big questions, nor let anyone else impose them on me. That I can't explain how the world came to be, or don't think a god made it does not mean that since I can't explain it, someone who can explain it with that god did it is more right than me. As far as I'm concerned, saying god did it is no better explanation than that nothing did it. All that religious conviction just seems arrogant. But maybe there is a god who did it, I don't know, and I don't need to know, and in the end I really don't care.

If I were an astrophysicist I might be pondering where the universe came from, but as a lay person and as an alcoholic it is sufficient for me to know that it is there. I don't need to make it any more complicated than that. The universe is there. And all the things in it are in it. And regardless of how much it is a wonder that the sun rises and bumblebees can fly, it is simply not my business to know whether it came to be this way because god made it so, or because of inherent laws in the universe, or whether by some infinitesimal chance it came to be so out of complete chaos. The bottom line still is I'm not in charge, and have every bit as much reason to be humble either way! Can I change the natural laws? Can I control chaos? I wasn't playing god. I just thought I had to do it all alone, and now I know I need help, and it's ok to ask my fellow recovering alcoholics for it.

But I have had to rewrite the whole program for myself, mostly by myself, and it has not been easy. I think it is finally coming together. God or no god, this is a spiritual program but let's keep it simple. It just consists of honesty, open-mindedness, willingness, humility, service, and living by the golden rule. It means doing the right thing, and if I work my program diligently, I will know what the right thing is, whether I pray for the knowledge for God's will for me or not, and if I do the right thing I will have no reason to drink, because I will be ok with me.

I have had to rewrite the steps for myself. I have to have faith that somehow this program will work for me, but that is all the justification for steps 2 and 3 that I have found. Some sort of personal inventory, and sharing it with another person is necessary, steps 4 and 5. The three elements of early AA, confession, restitution, and service, together with self examination are really the only essential elements in my program. And though they are rather Christian of origin, they work for me too, because and I am part of that Christian culture whether I believe in its god or not. Thinking along Christian lines comes easy to me since I grew up with it.

Self reflection does not come easy, though it is a prerequisite for growth. To actually come to think about what makes me tick, and if everything I think and do is right and just and for a good purpose in the greater scheme of things. Not just for my own selfish ends, but whether it makes the world at large a better place. It starts out a bit like the big question in the movie American History X: Has anything you have done made your life better?

Sure the AA fellowship has saved this alcoholic's life, though not because it is a higher power, but simply because of the love and help of the people in it, because together we can do what we could never do alone, like they say in another program's Unity "Prayer."

Sure I have seen a lot of people with a God who have had a much swifter recovery than me. Picking up the "ready made" toolkit has many advantages. However, having walked my own paths in this program I have had to turn every stone in my search for a spiritual life. And being forced to grope around on my own spiritually – and that has largely been the case for many years – looking back at it I think I have probably grown more, and in ways I otherwise never would have, if I had just taken on some sort of ready made Christian god concept and gone with it. All the answers and concepts a Christian can take for granted in this program, I have had to ponder deeply, and that, like any spiritual exercise, has given me much good growth. So I'm quite content with the course of my own recovery. I'm very grateful for all I have learned within or from AA these last 25 years.

* * *

The backlash against non-believers in AA that I have observed in recent years, including the White Paper, has made me realize the extent to which AA has become fossilized.

We as a fellowship need to take inventory, and when we are wrong promptly admit it. Instead the Big Book has become scripture, and the god people resist any change. For most of my time in AA I lived by a "Don't Tell" policy, but I have had to come out of the closet, as it were, and say out loud I'm an agnostic. I have put together a freethinkers meeting here in my area and I've met more closed-mindedness and unwillingness every step of the way. I fought the local Intergroup for 14 months to have the meeting listed in the schedule and lost.

The bright spot in all of it is that I have once again, like when I first got sober, found others like myself – this time at the AA Agnostica website, and books and other support material to go along with it. I once again no longer have to feel alone. It is giving me the courage to pick up the responsibility I have toward all the alcoholic non-believers that come into AA to let them know they can stay sober in spite of the god stuff, if they just keep showing up.

My first sponsor, incidentally a devout catholic, told me two things – that I heard, anyway: One was don't ever stop going to meetings, and the other was that service work will keep you sober when nothing else will. Sometimes my program is reduced to that. It's nice and uncluttered, and it has worked up to now. Let's keep this program simple.

18. Ann's Story

Ann M.

Already in kindergarten I felt different from others. I often felt ashamed and that I couldn't do things right. I mostly felt disliked throughout school, sometimes because I was the teacher's pet, sometimes because I would treat other kids badly to compensate for how I felt. I was also a crybaby.

But I was an avid reader, and always did well throughout school.

I went to college for a year, met the man I married at the start of my second year, and we married over Xmas. The idea that I could have sex when I wanted appealed to me greatly. Before meeting my husband I had dated a man who always seemed to know what I was thinking, and I found that scary. My husband, on the other hand didn't know, and didn't understand me. I liked that.

I was not the kind of drunk that crossed an invisible line sometime. I was already across it by the time I had my first drink. My family went to dinner to celebrate my 16th birthday, and I have no memory of what I wore, what I ate, who all was there, or what birthday presents I received, but I sure do remember the whiskey sour my Dad let me have. I spent the evening desperately trying to come up with some way to talk him into letting me have another. I drank rarely, but every time I did, I always wanted more.

Early on I was often able to have one and stop, but I always obsessed about wanting more. Every time I could have as much as I wanted, I did, and had frequent blackouts. The first blackout I actually knew I had had was when my husband and I had drinks before dinner, wine with dinner, and drinks after dinner. I knew we were going to make love, when we started drinking. The next thing I knew it was morning, and I couldn't remember anything beyond the wine at dinner. I never figured out a cool way to ask, "Did we have fun last night?"

Our marriage got rocky after our third child was born. I suffered through a number of suicidal depressions, which, of course, my husband did not understand. I had had depressions since child-hood. I was trying to figure out how to kill myself by age nine. I once asked my husband if I could see a psychiatrist, and he said he would rather divorce me and let me figure out how to support the kids and myself. I often thought about killing both the children and myself, but luckily I never tried to do it.

At Christmas time my depressions would be even worse. Every Christmas, I made all sorts of things for everyone in the family, but I always wound up in a deep depression for what I had not completed. I was a "glass-half-empty" sort of person – even for quite some time after sobriety. My Dad always preached that anything worth doing was worth doing perfectly. My motto seemed to be anything worth doing was worth overdoing. The severe depressions continued, getting worse and I used alcohol to treat them.

After I got sober in 1975 I realized at least part of my depression had been related to prescription weight loss medication which contained mood altering chemicals and that got worse once my doctor wouldn't prescribe any more and I was in withdrawal.

Meanwhile I suspected that my husband was molesting our daughters. Eventually I walked into the kitchen just as he kissed our 18 year old daughter in a definitely erotic manner. I felt unable to do anything about it, but wanting to be there for my daughters kept me from killing myself entirely with alcohol.

A friend from the Unitarian church had called me which had occasioned my latest attempt to not drink. She knew that my middle daughter kept running away from home, and she wanted to suggest that she come to live with her for a while. I was drunk when she pulled up to meet me, and I turned and ran for the house, falling and skinning my knees in the process. She called me a couple of days later to say she did not understand and hadn't wanted to embarrass me. I was beginning to get honest, and told her I had been drunk.

My husband and I had been seeing a counselor at the Air Base, and a few weeks after this incident, afraid I might not make it through another weekend, I finally admitted to the counselor that I "might" have a problem with alcohol, and he gave me a list of the three available AA meetings in town. I was a few weeks sober by then – one more attempt not to drink. I went to AA the next night and have been sober since then.

After I stopped drinking, my marriage was going downhill rapidly, and my husband was trying to get me to drink again, while I was trying to get him to stop drinking. One night he offered to fix dinner and served a glass of my favorite wine with dinner. I pitched a fit and went to bed without eating.

I was told early on to get women's phone numbers so I worked up the courage and asked, but all three who were sober had excuses for not giving it to me. Finally I asked one to be my sponsor, and she agreed, and gave me her phone number. This was right before I was going to visit my parents in Oklahoma. I started to work with her after I came back, but I eventually had to let her go because she was coming on to me, but she did give me confidence to make it through the trip.

I went to some really good meetings in Oklahoma. My mother had called me when I was about two months sober and I was not home so I told her I was at a meeting. She asked, "A church meeting?" I said, "No, an AA meeting – I'm an alcoholic". She got off the phone quickly and called my sister in Chicago to ask what she had done wrong to make me an alcoholic. My sister, whose best friend was alcoholic, had been to open meetings with her and to some Al-Anon meetings, so she told her if she and Dad wanted to know, they should go to Al-Anon and they would tell her, knowing that was the hook that would get her there. So they went.

When I was nine months sober I moved away from my husband, and lived on what I made substitute teaching. By this time, my children were gone from home except my son and he was leaving for college. I had one time affairs with two different AA members, and a longer one with a third. It was glorious for about six weeks, and then I sunk into a really deep depression. One daughter had finished high school and started college, and the other had moved in with a boyfriend.

I found my second sponsor about the time I moved out of my home. She and I were visiting an AA member in the hospital and she asked me if I would like to talk. She asked me if I had a sponsor, and when I said "no" asked me if I wanted her to be my sponsor and in tears I said "yes". Her next question was whether I was suicidal. More tears and another "yes".

I had never told anyone about my suicidal thoughts until then. Then I admitted it only because the woman who became my sponsor that day asked me about it.

I had admitted to not believing in any God when I was maybe nine months sober and they all put me down for it. The only reason I didn't get drunk then was that a man stopped me after the meeting and told me he had just heard a speaker with quite a few years sobriety say he didn't believe in God. He told me to not listen to the doom sayers.

My sponsor said I needed to go to treatment. She called Livengrin in Pennsylvania and they said it would be about a week's wait. She asked me if I wanted my mother to come and stay with me until I got in, and then she called her for me. By this time, mother had been in Al-Anon for a year, so she made plane reservations and went to her meeting to ask if it was okay. When they heard I had asked for her, they said, "Go". I took a 4th and 5th step while in treatment, which was neither searching nor fearless. I did not even admit to the affairs.

I returned home to try to make the marriage work. About eight months later, my husband sued me for divorce. Six months after that the divorce was final. He remarried two months later.

I wanted to leave the area, and my sponsor and the counselor said it was a good idea, so I moved to Des Moines, Iowa. My son was nearby in college. I found work quickly, and kept applying for other jobs also, and ended up becoming an EKG tech.

I stayed with this job for three years, but my boss was a drunk who would sometimes call at night, slurring her words, and give orders contrary to what she had said before she left work. Sometimes, we got in trouble for not doing what she said, and sometimes for doing what she had said. Eventually I had enough and quit.

I had saved up enough money to make it through a counselor training program, so I spent the next year doing that. One of the requirements of entering the training program was to complete the 28 day treatment as a patient, except we went home at night. Among our assignments we had to ask help from three other people who had already been through the program. I was five years sober already, so I figured it didn't apply to me. They wanted me to ask for help from someone sober only a few weeks? So when I turned in my assignments they failed me and just waited until four days later I figured out I better go ask for help after all. Then I passed. Humility wasn't my strong suit in those days.

I spent the next 25 years working as a counselor, until I retired. There were several "geographicals" along the way, and a number of depressions, some severe enough to need antidepressants for a time, some suicidal. What kept me from going through with it was the devastation I had felt when a member of our group committed suicide. I could not do that to my group.

My son finished college with a double major in physics and math. My older daughter finished a two year assistant veterinary program and later returned to college and completed a bachelor's in micro-biology. The other daughter completed a GED. I have an excellent relationship with one daughter and my son, while the other daughter struggles with mental illness and addiction. My son is in his own 12 step program, and that makes our conversations easier. AA has taught me that the only way to make amends to my children is to listen respectfully to what they tell me and not argue or offer excuses.

In my 40 years sober, I have had both my parents and a sister eight years younger die. I have had several accidents with broken bones. I was fired from a job as director of a treatment center, and another job as a counselor. In spite of all, I have not tried drinking again. While I know the first sip or two would feel good, I never want to feel again that awful feeling of despair when I could not stop. The long term benefits of sobriety far outweigh any short term feel-good.

I started trying to get an AA meeting for agnostics and atheists started a couple of years ago, but could not find a place to hold it. Finally, in Oct, 2014, there were four of us interested, so we got together, and after a couple of false starts finally have found a nice, stable place to meet. We have had as many as 24 at the meeting, and now another group has formed agnostic group has formed nearby as well. We do not use prayers, but end with the responsibility pledge.

I finally have the support I have always needed.

19. My Journey

Neil F.

On the 12th of April 1986, I drove from Toronto to Montreal and spent the evening drinking with friends. The next day, I visited my son from my previous marriage and drove back to Toronto. During the drive, I broke into a cold sweat and started shaking. I felt I was losing control of my mind and body. I was filled with shame and fear and I concluded I could no longer stand the pain of living this way. Something had to change.

I remembered what my doctor had told me during a visit a few months before. I told him a bit about why I drank, when I drank and was semi-honest about how much I drank. He told me that if I ever thought about having another drink I should look into a program called Alcoholics Anonymous. At the time, I felt angry and humiliated. How insulting.

But here I was, just a few months later, in the same old pickle. Once again I had been drinking; once again I was paying the price. What was worse, my standby solution – quitting on my own – was once again a total failure. In a moment of desperation, I reached out for help; on April 21, 1986, I attended my first AA meeting. Thanks to the fellowship of AA and good inputs from other sources I have not had to pick up a drink since.

In retrospect, I had a problem with alcohol from the moment I had my first drink.

I was actually quite shy, did not feel like I fit in and wanted very much to be accepted. I was ashamed of who I was. While I was successful at almost every task I took on, I never felt competent and lived in fear of others figuring out that I was in over my head. Alcohol became my instant friend; it allowed me to relax, to be more outgoing, to be a part of life, and my fear could be put on hold. It was a key component of both my social and business life and I could not imagine being able to live a normal, successful life if I were not able to drink. It was this desire to fit in that always took me back to the first drink.

I was not a daily drinker. While there were occasions when I would drink several days in a row, it was more common that I would go several days without a drink. I was very focused on controlling myself and my life when I was not drinking but after taking a drink I lost all control of how much I would drink and what I might say or do.

I had quit several times on my own with success lasting up to several months. My downfall was always finding myself in a social situation where I convinced myself that to be accepted and to relax I had to take a drink. It seemed like all of my normal friends and business acquaintances drank. There was no one who shared my objective of not drinking.

AA offered a community of people that I could identify with and who shared the objective of not drinking and who in many cases had good long term sobriety. Not only were they sober, many of them were successful and they seemed to be happy. I wanted what they had. This community of like minded people, more than anything, was what was missing when I attempted to stop on my own.

But as an atheist, I really struggled with many of the 12 steps.

I do not see myself as being powerless over alcohol as in and of itself alcohol is just a chemical and has no real power to control me. It is my brain, not alcohol, that is the problem. I did not like life as it was and I found that at least in the beginning alcohol was a solution. Over time, alcohol became a habit; a solution to all problems. When I took a drink, I lost control but it was really my reaction to life and not alcohol that caused me to pick up that first drink.

When I came to AA, I suffered from a seemingly hopeless state of mind and body that always led me back to a drink. But, my experience since then has shown me that it was not a hopeless state; I could recover from this state and live a productive, meaningful life without alcohol.

The suggestion of using a Higher Power as an alternative to a god would have been fine except for the fact that when I read the Big Book it was quite clear that the expectation was that sooner or later I would come to my senses and accept the Christian God as my higher power. So, I don't have a Higher Power in a Big Book or 12 Step sense. There are many things in the world more powerful than me, but there is no individual or group that I am willing to grant control over my life. I gain helpful input from many sources including AA members, AA groups, AA books and literature,

Buddhist, philosophy, psychology and neuroscience texts but in the end I retain responsibility for what is a part of my recovery practice.

While I did not find a higher power, I did find hope that I could recover as I listened to the experience of other members and read the stories in the back of the Big Book.

In the beginning I tried very hard to pursue the coming to believe route; I went to church a few times, I read the bible, books by CS Lewis, the Koran, some Buddhist and Hindu Texts but it didn't work. As well, the "Fake It Till You Make It" approach seemed to contradict the recommendation that I get honest with myself.

Several books on Buddhism provided helpful insights into how to approach and respond to life. While I reject what I'd call the "woo" associated with claims such as rebirth and karma from past lives, I do find help in the "Four Noble Truths", the "Eight Fold Noble Path" and the "Ten Perfections" and meditation. To me, these teachings and practices outline an approach to understanding my dissatisfaction with life and a process to bring about changes that help me live a good, happy life today. They are not religious in nature nor are they about the supernatural. As a result, these teachings inform the way that I approach the twelve steps.

I do not use the word spiritual when I'm discussing my practice as I think that it is a word that carries too much baggage in AA. Many would conclude that I am talking about a religious experience or perhaps some new age experience so it's a term I don't use. Instead, by working my own version of the steps I am bringing about changes in the way that I approach and respond to life. In the past, I measured success in terms of money, power, position or prestige; today they are no longer high on my list. Today I am more concerned with my relationships with others. I want to avoid harming others while helping where I am able. I am no longer as selfish or self centred as I used to be. I'm a long way from becoming selfless but I have made improvements.

So how could an alcoholic who is an atheist, who does not admit to being powerless over alcohol, who does not recognize a higher power and who does not claim to have had a spiritual awakening get sober, stay sober and have good long term sobriety? First I did not want to die; I did not want to abandon my family and I was convinced that without change I would die. Second, I had the fellowship and the examples of recovering and recovered members that gave me hope. And third, when I could not accept the steps as written in the Big Book, I personalized them to create a process that I could follow and that has helped change me and reduced the likelihood of picking up that first drink.

My current personalized version of the steps is as follows:

1. We admitted that we suffer from a seemingly hopeless state of mind and body.

2. Came to believe that we could recover.

3. Became open to changes in how we approach and respond to life.

4. Made a searching and fearless inventory of ourselves.

5. Reviewed our inventory with another human being.

6. Became entirely open to change.

7. Humbly affirmed our desire to change.

8. Made a list of all persons we had harmed and became ready to make amends to them all.

9. Made direct amends to such people wherever possible except when to do so would injure them or others.

10. Continued to take personal inventory and when we were wrong promptly admitted it.

11. Sought through meditation to improve our understanding of ourselves, our practice and our progress.

12. Having changed as the result of these steps, we tried to carry this message to alcoholics, and to practice these principals in all our affairs.

Due to my fear of not fitting in, of not being accepted in AA, I was not open about my atheism when speaking in AA until after I wrote an article "Personalizing the Twelve Steps" that was published on AA Agnostica in January of 2013. This article was really my full disclosure of my atheism, my becoming totally honest. Prior to this, when addressing a particular step in a meeting, I talked honestly about how I did the step but I did not disclose the fact that I am an atheist.

My disclosure caused some pain, one person called me a few names, and one person fired me as his sponsor, some rolled their eyes when I spoke, but others realized that I hadn't changed and still accepted me.

Coming out allows me to be honest when discussing my program. I do not wish to convert of de-convert anyone but I think it is important that others understand and acknowledge that it is possible to become sober and have good long term sobriety in AA without believing in a god.

Just over a year ago, two other members and I started our "Beyond Belief" meeting. It is an open AA Meeting, does not include any prayer, and uses readings from the book "Beyond Belief" to stimulate discussion. It is a great meeting attracting a small number of atheists, agnostics and even a few theists. We focus on our recovery experience.

Today my life is far removed from that seemingly hopeless state I was in when I first came to AA.

20. AA Atheist

Hanje R.

Few residents are in treatment because they choose to be. Most of us are "invited" by the courts, our employers, our family or friends. I arrived in treatment May 6, 1981 via an intervention that included family, friends and my boss.

We study the disease model: "addiction is a disease with biological, neurological, and environmental origins." We learn about cross-addiction: "if a person is dependent on one substance, he is at high risk to develop dependence on any other addicting substance." The counselors tell us it is important to get in touch with our feelings. We learn the symptoms of alcoholism. We watch videos, hear lectures and attend classes and twelve step meetings. They tell us that if we don't change we will continue to suffer consequences: jails, institutions and death.

Lights out and final cigarettes are at midnight and we awaken early. Naps are not allowed. Neither are cassettes or cassette players. The residents share a pay phone and there is a ten minute limit on calls. We are responsible for our own laundry and women are expected to wear bras.

We stand in a cafeteria line three times a day, we do our own dishes and listen to people assigned to stand up and say things like: "My name is Peter, and I am a worthwhile person". "My name is Sarah, and I love myself." By night the cafeteria becomes an AA meeting or a screening room for videos starring Leo Buscaglia aka Dr. Love, or Father Martin on a tall, boxy TV set.

It doesn't take long to let the routine and rules guide my days. I make friends, do my work and I am on time for all my meetings. For the most part I learn to fly under the radar, and make the best of my situation. I attend group and individual therapy and AA meetings. I am a model "prisoner". We have in-house AA meetings, and, after several days, we are "allowed" to attend required AA meetings on the outside.

I try to embrace AA, but it is a struggle. When I look at the steps or hear them this is what I see/hear: one "spiritual awakening", one "power greater than", one "prayer and meditation", one "His", three "Him"s and four "God"s. That was all I saw. That was all I heard.

I ask a staff member how I am going to do this AA thing when I don't believe in God. She explains that "in AA a higher power can be anything at all. Some people consider their higher power to be their twelve-step group." I figure she is trying and I listen to what she has to say: "Your higher power can be anything. Your higher power can be a bar of soap."

Soap? She stuns me with her response. Life-long atheist that I am, even I find this appalling. How can a person who purports to believe in God be disrespectful enough to suggest that a higher power could be a bar of soap? For the time being I give up on that question. I don't want to hear that or anything like that ever again. I need a new approach to the whole God issue.

I know that there are AA meetings at the local Unitarian Universalist Church, the church of my childhood. I am convinced that if I attend a meeting there, everything will come clear to me. Unitarian Universalism is a faith tradition that encourages each individual to develop a personal faith. It draws from many different religions, in the belief that no one religion has all the answers and that most have something to teach us. I came to my atheist beliefs while growing up in the UU Church. It was a conscious decision and I was supported in my choice by my church family.

I deduce that if I can attend the AA meeting at the UU Church, I will find a whole roomful of like-minded people. I am sure that the meeting will be different and I will meet people who have successfully dealt with the questions I am asking about how to make AA work for me.

I am surprised to find this meeting is the same as every other AA meeting I have attended. Its location in the UU Church does not solve the issue of "God language". The words they use are the same. People's stories are the same. The lesson I learn here is that a twelve step meeting is a twelve step meeting is a twelve step meeting. It's about the meeting, not about where it is held.

For all my struggles with AA, I do intend to stay sober. Or at least most of the time there is a good possibility that I will try to stay sober. Part of my brain is absorbing everything. I understand addiction. I understand the disease model. I understand cross-addiction.

I see that the longer you drink, the more you can drink, until you can't any more. I get that we were all trying to achieve those early highs, and no longer able to, we consume more, we consume something different, we fail, and we have no other solutions. I understand that sobriety is probably the only way out of the cycle of drug and alcohol use. I even believe that AA is my best bet for living a sober life.

When I graduate from treatment, I move to a halfway house for 90 days and then into a house with four other sober women. I attend four meetings a week. I learn to "translate" the "God language" into something more acceptable to me. This translation is more like censorship, but it works for me. I come to terms with the idea that I can say the prayers and read the steps, because, after all, I am just quoting.

I meet wonderful, generous people in the rooms of Alcoholics Anonymous and I aspire to be one of them, even as I struggle with speaking at meetings. When I do speak, I talk very rarely of my atheism. When I do, I am told with condescension that I "will find a higher power eventually." I feel connected to people I meet in AA, but I always feel a distance from the words, and I always feel somewhat separate because of my understanding of the God piece, the spirituality piece, the higher power piece.

Over the years I become much more active in Alcoholics Anonymous. I work for three years as a psych tech in a treatment facility and often transport women from the house to meetings, which I often attend with them. I become more open in meetings about my atheism. I feel like I am offering the newcomer an opportunity to hear a woman who has long-term sobriety who didn't have to change or compromise her spiritual and religious beliefs to do it. I become a member of the Unitarian Universalist Association Addictions Ministry Team. I lead AA meetings at UUA General Assembly, and am variously secretary and treasurer at some of the meetings I attend locally. I start to become one of those people I admired in my early years in the program. I speak about atheism on my sobriety birthday, and when I see another member of the fellowship struggling with the God language.

It is not until a beloved member of my own family is in treatment, struggling with the very things that I had struggled with when I was in treatment, that I try my hand at writing my own version of the 12 steps. I'm not sure if it is helpful to him, but it empowers me even further.

Hanje's Version of the 12 Steps

1. We admitted we were powerless over alcohol – that our lives had become unmanageable.

2. Came to believe that we could be restored to sanity.

3. Made a decision to turn our will and our lives over.

4. Made a searching and fearless moral inventory of ourselves.

5. Admitted to ourselves and to another human being the exact nature of our wrongs.

6. Were entirely ready to have all these defects of character removed.

7. Humbly asked for our shortcomings to be removed.

8. Made a list of all persons we had harmed, and became willing to make amends to them all.

9. Made direct amends to such people whenever possible, except when to do so would injure them or others.

10. Continued to take personal inventory and when we were wrong promptly admitted it.

11. Sought to find peace and serenity and to be the best people we could be.

12. We tried to carry this message to other alcoholics and to practice these principles in all our affairs.

I attend the first We Agnostics, Atheists, and Freethinkers (WAAFT) AA convention in Santa Monica, California, in November, 2014. I find out that there are people all over the world that have been doing their own translations of the steps, have been hiding their own atheism, who have felt shamed, just like I did. I finally have a tribe. I stay in touch with these people on social media. I attend the Agnostics and Others Group of Alcoholics Anonymous meeting in my own community and I look forward to being reunited with my tribe when WAAFT meets in Austin, Texas, in 2016.

21. My Name is Marnin

Marnin M.

My name is Marnin and I'm an alcoholic and an agnostic/atheist. Marnin is Hebrew for he who brings joy, a singer of songs. In my youth I was embarrassed to have such an unusual name.

I have been sober for 44 years, since my first AA meeting on October 27, 1970, in Brooklyn.

AA saved my life, and I am forever grateful for the opportunities it has provided me. Because of the AA program and therapy, I try to live as full and as emotionally satisfying a life as possible.

What It Was Like

I was born in 1935, the only child of parents with poor nurturing skills. I was nervous as a child and my parents sent me to a Jewish private school. I felt like a square peg forced into a round hole then, and for the rest of my life, before AA.

My father rarely ever spoke with me. When my mother divorced him, my father blamed me for the breakup. I felt abandoned by my parents. To this day I often feel like an orphan and find it hard to remember that I had parents.

I muddled through high school and college socially inept and feeling lost.

The first time I felt "normal", like one of the boys, was in the Army. I liked that the army, my "Uncle Sam", was taking care of me. For the first time someone cooked for me on a regular basis.

I found the perfect place to work when you have little self confidence and self esteem – the garment industry in downtown New York.

At the age of 28, I got my own apartment and sort of accidentally threw explosive floor shavings into the incinerator. As a result of the explosion, I was rushed to King County Hospital.

It was at this time that my doctor, who was familiar with my family history, got me into therapy. I was a very angry young man. The only emotions I was in touch with with were anger and fear. I went into therapy a college graduate, a virgin, non-smoker, non-drinker, and fearful that I might be gay.

And it was in therapy that I began to drink. I discovered how angry I was with both my parents, particularly my mother. In order to quell the anger I would go from the doctor's office to a bar (Yaeger House) and meditate about what I was learning in therapy over a stiff martini.

I now had my magic solution to life's problems – therapy and alcohol. Within a year I was in a relationship and, with enough alcohol in me, lost my fear of intimacy. No longer a virgin at age 28 I had to make up for lost time. In my mind I set out to be a Jewish James Bond of the garment industry.

After being in therapy for seven years, a serious relationship with a girl I wanted to marry ended suddenly. I was crushed and crashed. I experienced the feelings of abandonment from this relationship that were part of my life as a result of my parents.

I became a full-blooded alcoholic, drinking 24 hours a day. I drank the way they describe in country music songs. I showed up for business trips without my airline tickets and all the other things that you hear in AA. Blackouts were frequent. I shudder at the thought of going through the Brooklyn Battery Tunnel often in blackouts and getting up at 2 a.m. to look for my car and be sure that their was no blood or damage from an accident I did not remember.

In 1969 I met a Jewish young lady and married her in ten days. My orthodox Jewish family had considered me dead because I had been living with a Christian girl. So I was married to a Jewish woman by a Rabbi and I was now kosher in their terms. The marriage was a disaster. I was in a blackout at our wedding because I knew I had made a terrible mistake.

I had my first detox soon after at Freeport Hospital in Long Island. They used the 12-Step program of AA at Freeport. I heard the Steps for the first time and decided they were Christian in nature and not for me. Needless to say I continued drinking. My therapist says that if you can't kill yourself, you marry someone who will do it for you. My wife literally tried to murder me and I went off to Mexico for a quickie divorce.

What Happened

My end came in October 1970 as a result of a suicide attempt that involved drinking, marijuana and thorozine. The thorozine had been prescribed because I had developed alcoholic neuropathy. I was having trouble walking without alcohol in my blood stream.

I had a terrible drunk/trip which ended with a vivid hallucination and "spiritual experience". I hallucinated Jesus on the cross bleeding all over me. Turns out it was my own blood. I heard Jewish music coming out of the walls. I lay there and realized that I was crucifying myself and that I did not want to die!

I called AA in New York. I told them AA wouldn't work for me because "I'm Jewish and a college graduate". The volunteer at Intergroup responded with "Maybe we can help you anyway".

I joined AA on October 27, 1970. AA was the only lifeboat around so I climbed aboard.

My first home group was the Brooklyn Heights group. Coming into the rooms of AA, I perceived it to be a religious program and that is still how I view it. I looked for answers in the 12 Step program and, not believing that God intervenes in human affairs, I put the whole God thing aside and followed my own secular version of the Steps.

AA was my "religion". When I was two or three months sober an Episcopalian Minister in Brooklyn Heights defined religion as the three B's and it saved my life: Believing that AA will help me stay sober; Behaving as a responsible person and going to any length to stay sober; Belonging to a fellowship that rooted for me to stay sober.

In the 1970s, it was thought that Jews couldn't be alcoholics. The same Minister pulled out a Jewish copy of a Biblical proverb and I knew then I could be Jewish and have a disease from the Old Testament:

> Who has woe? Who has sorrow?
> Who has strife? Who has complaining?
> Who has wounds without cause?
> Who has redness of eyes?
>
> Those who linger long over wine.
> Those who go to taste mixed wine.

Do not look on the wine when it is red,
When it sparkles in the cup and goes down smoothly;
At the last it bites like a serpent
And stings like an adder.

Your eyes will see strange things
And your mind will utter perverse things.

And you will be like one who lies down
In the midst of the sea, on top of a mast.
They struck me, you will say, and I was not hurt.
They beat me, you will say, but I did not feel it.

When will I awake?
So I can seek yet another drink.

AA was my home base for sobriety. Most of my life I've fought the feeling that I was not good enough. This feeling sometimes over-whelmed me and it is what precipitated my final drunk. I found in AA what I had been looking for in the bottle: I was welcomed by total strangers and experienced from them the warm feelings and concern that most children receive from loving parents. Nurturing: this was what I had been looking for in the bottle. I found it in AA.

The "B" of Belonging means to me being active in AA, sharing, attending and chairing meetings. Sometimes even going to a meeting when I don't want to.

Because of how I work the program I have not always been the most popular person in AA, and some have told me that I am not doing it the "AA way".

It's not surprising to me then that when members first choose to come out of the closet about their real beliefs about GOD they whisper it to me like they are guilty of a great sin. I share this message today partly in the hope that other nonbelievers will find strength in knowing that they are not alone and can still, as I did, find sobriety in AA.

I went to any length to stay sober and immersed myself in AA. I was assured my life without alcohol would change dramatically and it did!

What It's Like Today

It was only after joining AA that I started using my real name, Marnin. Having escaped death I felt free to use my real name. I was no longer embarrassed by a unique name. Sober in AA I felt I had earned the right to be me. For my first anniversary instead of a medallion I had an ID bracelet made with my name engraved on it in Hebrew.

Since sex without alcohol was new to me I acted like a tomcat. I had another spiritual awakening this first year and discovered I could no longer act like this and live with myself.

I met my wife Fran at Grossingers Resort singles week in the Catskill Mountains in my first year of sobriety. We have a daughter Lisa who is still finding her self. Unfortunately she eats like I drank. Since I identify with her addiction I want to "fix" her. I am learning that we are powerless over her illness and all we can do is be there for her and be loving, nurturing and supportive parents.

My years of sobriety are the happiest I have ever had. AA's 12 steps, as I have understood and worked them, have provided me with a tool box for living that allows me to try to be the best Marnin I am capable of being, one day at a time. When we left New York and moved to Florida in 2003, I had been very active in the Promises Group in Nyack, NY. I booked institution talks for my group and was very active getting members to speak. I still sponsor and correspond with my AA friends back in New York. I've also created an AA speakers CD library for the group and for Open Arms, the local half way house.

I am presently an active member of the Sunday morning Tequesta, Florida Beachcombers Group Meeting. I am known as the CD man, always pitching portable sobriety in the form of AA and Al-Anon speaker CDs. Some call this my "ministry". I call it part of my twelfth Step.

During my years of sobriety I've tried to be open and honest and to practice the 12 Steps in all my affairs. Many have told me that I talk about things that should not be talked about. I say "malarkey". If it is part of my story, I talk about it!

I have answered phones at Stuart Intergroup Office for almost ten years, since I first arrived in Florida. They know here that I am an agnostic and don't care. I guess they must think I am doing something right.

From my first day of sobriety, Alcoholics Anonymous has been my loving, accepting family.

Thank you. My name is Marnin.

Editor's Note: Thirty-five years ago an aspiring writer in group therapy with Marnin wrote this wonderful poem about him:

> Like a sailor ashore after a long and stormy voyage,
> Marnin walks with exaggerated care,
> expecting the earth to roll and toss him off balance.
> He scans the sky looking for thunderclouds to brighten his day,
> and shivers in the sun.
>
> Prepared for tempests, he stows his joy and battens down his life,
> so he won't be washed away.
> But the sea change has rooted, the gales passed.
>
> It is the calms Marnin must weather, to avoid drifting
> into whirlpools of anticipation.
> Fear-fogged, snug in his own cool shadow,
> only the heat of his passions can melt the mists in which he hides.

22. Positive Attitude Changes Everything

Helen L.

My name is Helen and I am an alcoholic. That simply means that I cannot safely drink. I have been introducing myself at Alcoholics Anonymous meetings that way for 30 years.

I came into the rooms at age 23 having been kicked out of college for failing to maintain grades. I had been an honors student and I was devastated by my repeated failures semester after semester. A psychiatrist in recovery introduced me to my first AA meeting. He told me before we walked in: take what you need and leave the rest. I have never forgotten that advice. He also wrote in a Big Book for me: Positive Attitude Changes Everything.

Although I recognized that my life was unmanageable, I did not know if I was really an alcoholic. There were always more notorious drinkers around me to prove otherwise. I was in the early stages of the disease: periodic embarrassing binges, punctuated by occasions where I could manage to have just one. However, I couldn't predict when that would be. And those controlled drinking occasions were becoming less and less frequent over time. I was less and less reliable at school, procrastinating with my own to-do lists, missing classes, not meeting my own potential. My religion of origin had given me plenty of beliefs about God, but by the time I had been kicked out of college, I had lost faith in myself.

I kept coming back to meetings because I wanted what the people in AA clearly had: they had turned their lives around from failure to success, they were no longer ashamed of themselves, they were happy. I was willing to abstain – temporarily – from alcohol while I learned their secret to achieving serenity.

They did not kick me out for not knowing whether or not I was one of them.

Eventually I heard other women tell my story. I read on page 23 in the Twelve Steps and Twelve Traditions these words granting us early stage alcoholics admission into the fellowship:

(We) were joined by young people who were scarcely more than potential alcoholics. They were spared that last ten or fifteen years of literal hell the rest of us had gone through... How could people such as these take this step (one)?

By going back over our drinking histories, we could show that years before we realized it we were out of control, that our drinking even then was no mere habit, that it was indeed the beginning of a fatal progression...

Alcoholism was progressive! I went over my own relatively shorter drinking history and found that it indeed had been getting worse over time. That night was my first time identifying in as an alcoholic.

There were in the rooms holy roller Big Book thumpers whose angry zealotry was unattractive to me. But the majority of AA members welcoming me in 1985 were extremely accepting of people not like them. They practiced live and let live and unconditional love. This is the most important modeling AA has ever given me. We were diverse in terms of gender, races, classes, ages, abilities, diagnoses, politics, beliefs, sexual orientations. None of that mattered. Our recovery together came first.

I was still very sensitive to criticism. Being judged, for any reason, would have chased me back out those doors. I was lucky to have stumbled into the one place of acceptance and unconditional love that would eventually heal not only my alcoholism but also my own self-judgment, projection and shame issues.

Because I was attracted to the remarkable serenity in AA, I embarked on the steps – and attempted to use the conception of god that I had been taught in my youth. I did my best but did not feel any lightning bolts of closeness to a higher power as claimed by some of our religious members. I attributed this disappointment to some fault of my own. Nevertheless, I stayed sober and kept coming back. I placed myself into the middle of the boat, and my social life included mostly people in recovery.

My initial sponsor was a mother figure to me. But when the time came to take my 4th & 5th steps, well, there are some things one cannot tell one's mother. So I asked another woman whom I had heard joyfully leading a 10th step meeting if she would help me start my 4th step. I wanted the joy she had experienced in practicing self-examination. "I am happy to help you! Your 5th step is with me next week." This was not what I expected to hear, but the immediate 5th step deadline was exactly what I needed to focus and complete step four. I learned to look wherever pride and fear could trip me up. Her own nonjudgement and her guidance away from self-judgement was such a revelation to me. I had been swimming in a soup of perfectionistic judgmentalism all my life. Free of self-judgment, I was then free to become more understanding of myself and of others.

Through my trust in the principles of program, my connection to others who were working the steps, and my willingness to apply these principles in my own life, I have become more able to "live life on life's terms", to feel more comfortable in my own skin, and to overcome other issues besides alcohol.

My work on letting go of attempting to control the disturbing behaviors of other people brought me into other fellowships. So I also learned "inner child" lessons about myself and detachment issues about life from Alanon and Adult Children of Alcoholics.

I learned boundaries: for instance, not to tolerate intolerable behavior from others. I learned I could just acknowledge how I was feeling and ask for what I needed rather than telling bad actors exactly what I thought of them. If they weren't willing to improve their relationship with me, I was free to focus on better relationships elsewhere. I accept that some relationships teach us valuable lessons, and that we can sometimes outgrow people. I have learned to "Go where you are celebrated, not where you are tolerated (or denigrated)".

I was also able to turn my life around into successful living in more tangible ways.

Early on, I returned to complete my college degree and later I went on to obtain a Master's Degree in Social Work and had a successful career as an employee assistance counselor and clinical social worker. And, years later, after I married, I also became a Master Gardener, a beekeeper, and a Permaculture Designer.

I have raised a lovely daughter who is now starting college. She has always known me as a sober mother, and along with her father, also sober, we provided a stable home. During her high school years, I was hired to teach college courses in Horticulture. I had come full circle from being expelled from college in my 20's to becoming a college associate professor in my fifties. I was meeting my potential and becoming my own best self.

As our literature promises, more has been revealed. My long-time immersion in a loving, accepting and sober atmosphere eventually resulted in a change in my conception of a power greater than myself. I now view this greater power not as a divine personage but as a human interconnective flow of love and service between all of us.

I've been a newbie atheist for almost five years. I went through a dark night of the soul to get here. To transition from believer to nonbeliever is a frightening process. Abandonment issues needed to be resolved first.

I do acknowledge a power "greater than myself": Lovingkindness is very powerful. It encompasses all of us and includes me. I strive to be non-hierarchic in all things. I still practice the steps to maintain honesty, open-mindedness and willingness and I appreciate the self-examination wisdom in them.

For myself, I translate the word God wherever it appears in the literature to the word Lovingkindness. In step 3, I dedicate myself to practicing the principle of Lovingkindness. Although I can still speak fluently the language of Christian philosophy, I identify today as an atheist in the rooms. I accept graciously that others are not there yet. It took me two decades to graduate up to atheism, who am I to judge anyone for where they are now in their 2nd step journey? Besides, I know from personal experience that this program works either way, both with belief in a deity and without. So our beliefs do not really matter. It is faith in the loving power at work among people in these rooms that matters. As the literature still reminds me, "This is the way to a faith that works".

As Ebby T. suggested to Bill Wilson long ago, we are free within Alcoholics Anonymous to choose our own conceptions of a power greater than ourselves. We can live our beliefs and let others live theirs. Our common welfare in recovery comes first. Lovingkindness: This is the way to a faith that works. Positive Attitude Changes Everything.

23. The Power is in the Process

John C.

I started drinking at 30 years old. This was because my father was an alcoholic. He was not a bar drinker, but he came home every night and terrorized the family. At 14 years old I made a personal oath to never drink. I went to college, grew my hair long, was an art student, and played guitar in a psychedelic rock band, but using alcohol or drugs was something I never did. Back in the 1960s it was assumed that anyone, with long hair and who played guitar, drank a lot or was on some kind of drug. No one ever questioned me about my secret personal oath.

In my 20s I had odd jobs and obsessed over playing scales correctly on guitar. At that time in my life I didn't perform as a musician, I was just fascinated by the mathematics of music.

At 30 years old I moved to San Francisco, far from where my father had died five years before, and one day someone handed me a drink. I guess I felt sufficiently separated from my earlier non-drinking life, and my fathers drinking, so I had my first drink.

Drinking had an immense affect on me. I felt like I had died and gone to heaven. I became a daily drinker on the day of my first drink. I could now look people in the eye and with my new found confidence I got a good job.

I was working as an electronic technician, drinking until late at night and then, with no hang-over, going into work the next day. Sometimes I would be in a black-out until 10 AM. I would "wake-up" at my desk at work or out in the field repairing equipment. But everyday at 5 PM I would start to shake and sweat and I knew I had to get a drink as soon as possible. It was a strange lifestyle, but I felt it came with the territory of me now being a drinking man, something I could never see giving up.

This went on for three years until my first AA meeting. My boss at work called me into his office around 5 PM one day and in the silence we could hear the ice rattling in my soda cup. He told me I had to get my act together. Then a girlfriend told me that she had been to Al-Anon and they told her I should go to AA. So I went.

My first impression of the meeting was good. People were laughing and telling wild stories. As I sat in the meeting I could feel my attitude and perspective changing. I was identifying with the stories. By the end of the meeting I thought this was really cool, I belonged here, and I didn't want to drink anymore.

But then I looked up on the wall and saw the 12 steps, god this and god that. I was an atheist and my heart fell, this was never going to work for me.

I became an atheist in the third grade when I was sent to Catholic school. I didn't believe anything they were telling me. I was a reader of Popular Science magazine and to this day I believe that everything has a scientific explanation.

I left that first meeting with AA members chasing after me, telling me they were positive there was a god and I needed to believe in him. I thought I would never return. After a short home detox I didn't drink for two weeks, but then started drinking again.

For the next three years I would try to prove that I could fix myself. I tried Antabuse, but drank on it. I had two drunk-driving arrests and also spent a couple of nights in drunk tanks. Once my job sent me out of town where I ended up in the local drunk tank. The owner of the business I was working with had to bail me out. I even went back to AA meetings a few times, with no intention of working the steps, but to get that collective spirit of not drinking. It would give me a week or two of drying out. One time I realized that I was about to have 30 days, but drank on the 30th day because I didn't want any official connection to people who believed in the supernatural.

Finally in March of 1982 I was on a nasty drunken weekend and was fired from a job the following Monday. I had drank that morning and I went into work drunk. I was sick and tired of being sick and tired.

At AA meetings I had heard that, "The only requirement for AA membership is a desire to stop drinking." This was the key. After a four day home detox I marched into an AA meeting with the idea, "This AA thing does not have to be about belief". I am somehow going to make this work.

Having gone to meetings off and on for three years I could see the science behind how the program worked. People use god-belief when they don't understand what is really going on. The AA program with its meetings and 12 steps works very well, but the majority of members are under the delusion that a supreme being has cured them of alcoholism. When I realized that I could utilize the program without having to follow this philosophy of god-belief, I felt a new freedom.

Carl Jung the Swiss psychiatrist had used the term "collective unconscious" and when I heard that term I knew right away what it meant. Once when I was in college we had an impromptu snow-ball fight with 200 students that ended up out on the main highway through town. Here I was in the middle of a major highway blocking traffic and throwing snow-balls at cars. This was something I would never do on my own, but in the group of students it felt like the natural thing to do. I remembered back to my first AA meeting where this same feeling of power came over me. My unconscious connection to the group changed my thinking. And the fact that I didn't intentionally change my own thinking is why this process is called a spiritual experience. It was something happening that was beyond my control.

Within two months I was on a pink cloud. I was going to meetings everyday and had many AA friends. At one year a sponsor found me. He accepted that I was an atheist.

Step 2 for me was seeing that people were getting sober in AA. The power greater than myself was the effect of the AA group and the AA process. It was the cause and effect of identifying at meetings and working the steps, a natural phenomenon within the realm of human behavior.

Step 3 for me at that time was religious talk, but I understood it to be an affirmation of moving forward with my life. Starting to do a 4th step was an indication that I had accepted the 3rd step.

With my sponsor I did a 4th and 5th step. This brought about a real sense of freedom and a feeling of belonging in the AA fellowship.

At two years sober I also joined Overeaters Anonymous and at that point I realized what Steps 6 & 7 were about. We need to get into action to get rid of our character defects.

Making Step 9 amends was painful, but inevitably very healing.

Also at 2 years sober I got a job working as a technician on a movie project that took place in a winery up in Napa Valley, California. On the first day the director of the movie announced that anyone could have a free bottle of wine everyday after work. I was suddenly struck by the fact that I didn't have the desire to drink any wine and here it was even free wine. Something had happened to me over the past two years that completely changed my attitude and perspective.

I met my wife Linda when I was still drinking. After I was sober a year we got married. Being in a relationship is where I quickly learned about the 10th step. I needed to make amends whenever it was necessary to maintain a happy family.

I never really thought about step 11 until I was 20 years sober. It has such a religious tone it seemed unnecessary. But I realized that it was about us being happy, joyous and free. We need to get an idea about what action is necessary for us to be happy, joyous and free. Sometimes it is helping others, but it could also be going back to school or taking a few classes in something we are interested in. Today I go to a weekly AA meditation meeting.

At three years sober Linda and I moved to Los Angeles where for 20 years I worked in a business I had always wanted to work in. We even had an AA meeting on the lot where I worked. I sponsored other alcoholics and for 23 years answered phones at our AA central office. I always enjoy the opportunity to explain the AA program to other atheists.

We raised two daughters who grew up with program parents. Someone asked one of our young daughters once what an alcoholic was and she responded that alcoholics were people who went to meetings. We have had many 12 step program friends over the years and many wonderful social gatherings.

In Los Angeles I also found an AA meeting called We Agnostics. It had been started in 1980 by an alcoholic named Charlie P. Most atheists dislike the AA Big Book chapter We Agnostics, but Charlie said he chose that title so the meeting would get listed at Central Office.

The meeting was very raucous and high spirited with around 40 people attending. My first time there I heard someone shout out, "I don't read the Big Book and I don't trust anyone who does!" Wow! That was a refreshing change from other meetings I thought. Many of the AA members there had long-term sobriety. For many years now this and other We Agnostics meetings have been an interesting gathering spot for us sober freethinkers and a nice relief from the god-believing meetings.

I am now retired, but still work at many creative projects. Linda and I still enjoy going to AA, Al-Anon, and other 12 step meetings.

I believe that we all get sober with the same power greater than ourselves, but myself and many others don't see that power coming from supernatural beings or divine intervention. The power is in the process. The power is in the process. What got me sober was the experience of meetings, the action of inventory, amends, and service, and the spirituality of the human spirit.

24. Utter Desperation

Alice B.

Nothing could have brought me to Alcoholics Anonymous other than utter desperation and the lack of any viable alternative. I started drinking when I was twelve years old, despite growing up in a supportive family where no one really drank. We were not religious. We were not alcoholics. Nothing about AA fit our profile. By October 15th 2007, the last time I took a drink, AA had become my last resort. Two stints in rehab had helped me learn a lot of things about addiction and about myself, but didn't keep me sober for long. The problem with rehab was maintenance. In order for me to get my first consecutive three months of sobriety, I really had to do "90 meetings in 90 days" and the only place I knew to get that was in AA. What AA gave me was access almost anytime, anywhere to other alcoholics who had come to believe that getting sober was worth doing anything to get, that getting and staying sober is – anyone new and struggling may find hard to believe – entirely possible and, as I learned, actually much easier than drinking.

If it weren't for the overt religious aspects of AA, I might have been spared years of suffering.

I was deeply alienated by AA's reputation for religiosity and it really kept me away. When I started going to meetings, I was more embarrassed someone would see me outside a church than an AA meeting. Time and again I met sponsors who wouldn't let me get past step two because I could not in honesty say I was willing to "give my life over to God". The slogan that goes with that step is "Let Go and Let God". Ironically, it's the first part of that slogan, "letting go", that helped me find a way to be in AA. All I had to do was let go of the second part, the "let God" part, to "take what I needed and leave the rest".

Finally I could sit in meetings and not get hung up every time God became the central topic. I could use those times to meditate, and read the Big Book for the parts that worked for me. After all, the only goal was to stay sober. Getting angry, feeling chased out of meetings because of my lack of religious beliefs, these things would get in the way of sobriety, so I had to let them go. What I learned about letting go in meetings, I could apply to my life outside of meetings. I'm not the first to say that meetings are a kind of microcosm where you can experience and work through feelings and reactions that will help you outside meetings. The advantage in meetings is that you can try out new emotions without professional or social repercussions. But being sober also has given me choices, and today I choose to attend meetings where there is less God talk and more sober talk. In fact, in most countries where I attend meetings, there is a much more secular approach to AA.

For decades, there was not a day I wasn't either drunk or hung over. Drinking that much is like living life with a ball and chain that you have tied around your own ankle. Thinking back, it's astonishing I accomplished what I did. It's astonishing I did not get myself killed. Nearly every terrible thing that happened to me happened when I was drunk. There is a whole category of "sex with strangers" stories I could tell, but they are so standard and tawdry that they don't need telling. Every drunk I know has similar stories.

I thought that alcohol was freedom, my constant companion, my friend in foreign places, my antidote to loneliness. But alcohol was the lousiest kind of friend: it was jealous and possessive and stripped me of who I could be. It belittled me, shamed me, hurt me. If alcohol was my lover, I was alcohol's battered spouse.

After my six years at university (something of a respite from the worst of my drinking) I got a job in the film industry, where, at least at that time, and at least in the department I worked in, drinking was a big part of the lifestyle. Sometimes when a shoot ended in the morning, we were rewarded with beer. I was in heaven. It's worth saying that I never had any trouble keeping up with "the boys". We worked hard and partied hard and that excused us for everything.

It was around that time I went to my first AA meeting. I'd come home with a guy I'd picked up in a booze can (an all night illegal drinking club). He had a cell phone, which was still a new thing. I used his cell phone to leave myself a phone message that said, "You need help". I was still too drunk that morning to find AA in the phone book, but the next day I made it to a meeting. I didn't make it my second AA until two years later.

In the meantime, I moved to Cambodia to kick-start a career as a photojournalist and, I thought, to get away from my boozy life in Toronto. I'd left home at 16 so I wasn't new to the concept of a "geographic": where you think that moving to another city will help you escape demons that, as it turns out, you carry with you every-where you go. Working in conflict zones, as a war correspondent, was another career that pretty much gave me impunity over drinking alcoholically. But it also made me feel guilty knowing I was dishonoring the work and the people whose stories I was meant to be telling. Moreover, the crippling, soul-shattering hangovers I suffered meant I was rarely on my best game. I would not have admitted it then, but being hung-over didn't just put my life in danger, but also the lives of my colleagues and everyone around me.

Cambodia was an incredible experience, and it did set me on a new career path. But this path was rife with roadblocks and potholes created by my drinking. I rediscovered uppers. Now I learned how to combine cocktails of uppers with booze that enabled me to prolong my drinking and somehow manage to get to my job teaching English as a Second Language the next morning at 6 am. Then I'd hop on my motorcycle and cover the day's news, before going back to the bar at night and starting the cycle all over again. Many nights after all the other customers had gone, the only souls left at the bar were me and the hookers. Increasingly, I was doing more drinking than working. I had motorcycle accidents, lost job opportunities, hung out with junkies and prostitutes. I earned the nickname "Calamity Jane". On the outside it was still a big party, a wild adventure, but on the inside I was dying. It was unsus-tainable.

One day I met a guy about my age who became a quick drinking buddy and friend. "Jack" had once been sober for a whole year. My eyes were wide with amazement: "How did you do that?" I wanted to know. He told me he'd been in rehab in New York, and that that year sober was the best year of his life.

I'd never forgotten what Jack had told me. He'd put the idea in my head that it was possible to stop drinking – something I desperately needed to believe. Sitting at a lake-side bar drunk, at 10 o'clock in the morning, I scrawled a note in my journal admitting that I had a problem and that I could no longer deny the selfishness and insanity that was preventing me from doing something more worthwhile with my life. A few weeks later I flew back to Toronto and checked into my first rehab. I then planned on moving to New York and, among other things, reconnecting with my friend Jack. I wanted to tell him about rehab, about how he'd helped me get there. But before I made it to New York, Jack died of a heroin over-dose.

I went to my first rehab in 1999. In between that time and my second rehab I still wanted to believe I wasn't really an alcoholic. My second stint in rehab was in 2005 after I'd spent two years covering the war in Iraq and had fully relapsed. I did not last 12 hours sober that time. All it took was my boyfriend dumping me the night I got back from rehab and I was off on a two-day bender with a stranger I met at a bar. It took me two more years to get back into AA after that.

AA advises us to avoid "emotional entanglements" in our first year of sobriety. Truth be told, I still have to be careful about emotional entanglements. That also means avoiding people who are "toxic" to me. When I got honest about it, I was able to see which relation-ships were healthy and which relationships were feeding my addic-tions. I've cleaned house massively and now surround myself only with people around whom I feel I am my best self or am inspired to be my best self – someone I can like when I look in the mirror because I know she is trying to do the best she can.

How often I realized I'd totally screwed up my day! I would be left in a drunken fog between being awake and being asleep. My mind was too far gone to think but not tired enough to sleep. Today when I "remember when" it's those times I remember as the worst. You are imprisoned in a mind you cannot stand being inside anymore and there is nowhere to go because you can't escape yourself. In was an unbearable place to be and I despised myself for letting it happen. And yet I repeated it over and over again.

Drinking didn't make anything better. Grey days were exponentially greyer. Cold days were interminably colder. Extremely hot days were insufferably hotter. Nothing ever felt right. Discomfort was the standard and everything I tried to do to drink myself out of discom-fort stopped working. I don't know if it ever worked. Back when I was a teenager in Toronto, one of my best friends called me up to take me for beers across the street. It was a school night, but he insisted. We drank Amsterdam beer, which was a bit fancy back then. The next day he killed himself by jumping off the Millwood Bridge. Looking back, I can't help but wonder what role alcohol played in his inability to see past his problems. His death was a big turning point for me too: I now used it as an excuse to get obliterated whenever I felt like it. I don't know if the horrible feeling I got in my gut the moment I heard what had happened left me until I was well into my first year of sobriety. Every shitty thing that happened thereafter just added to it. That is what happens when you drink your troubles away: every bad feeling is added to the previous bad feeling. You can no longer distinguish the cause of one bad feeling from the next.

When my feelings started coming back to me after some time in sobriety and AA, it was almost unbearable at first. I sat in meetings for months just crying. If I hadn't had AA meetings to go to every day and someone to talk to every day, I wouldn't have been able to stand it. I read the AA literature with gusto, looking for ways to proceed, ways to cope with my feelings, ways to make the unbearable bearable, ways to feel less alone and less ashamed. I would say the slogans over and over again: grant me the serenity to accept the things I cannot change, the courage to change the things I can and the wisdom to know the difference; one day at a time; this too shall pass; do the next right thing and let go of the outcome. I would wish for serenity and joy for anyone I had any resentment or anger toward. When I wished for it hard enough, I realized I really did want them to be happy. That was a revelation that went a long way to work out my own pent up anger.

I was forced to deal with my emotions and look at my part in things that had hurt me or the hurt I had caused others. Somehow, recognizing the choices I'd made and taking accountability helped me hate less. One morning I woke up and for the first time in memory, since my friend's suicide, I did not have a horrible feeling of dread in my stomach. Since then, I continue to do whatever I can to keep that feeling away. After a while, something really amazing started to happen: Whenever that bad feeling came back, I was able to identify it as a sign that something was wrong. For the first time I understood the expression, "to have a gut feeling". Now, when I "have a bad feeling about something", I listen to myself. I assess the situation, I do my research, and more often than not I am able to avert a problem or danger because of that feeling. Our emotions are a compass for living. Even the bad ones are worth having and listening to!

Even when I was drinking, I could see that the artists and writers who really were at the top of their game (with very few exceptions) did not abuse alcohol. They were too busy being engaged in their work. My own creative output has gained a clarity and depth that would have been impossible when I was drinking (not to mention that it is unlikely I would still be alive if I hadn't stopped drinking).

I still have bad days occasionally, but they are few and far between. Bad days used to drag into years. Now I have what is sometimes called "an emotional relapse", where my emotions become overwhelming and I allow myself to give in to either an episode of rage or grief. Or I'll pick a fight with someone. It's usually connected with being hungry, angry, lonely or tired. The difference is that I am able to stop, to walk away, to figure out what to do next. It's not like a drink, where once you start you cannot stop. When I drank, there were times I believed I would not be able to survive the bad feelings I had. Drinking was the only way to survive, until drinking didn't work anymore.

Today, no matter how terrible I may feel, I know that I'll get past it. I do this by start with "do the next right thing", which is what I had written on my first year medallion. Sometimes that means: stop arguing, or just leave, or take a break. My ability to love and forgive others seems to be inextricably tied to my ability to love myself. A good night's sleep can turn things around. What a concept! Rest and heal your mind rather than go out and beat the crap out of yourself with poison so that the next day you will wake up feeling even more horrible and hostile.

The very important second part of "do the next right thing" is to "let go of the outcome". That frees me up to move on to doing "the next right thing" again, and on and on, like that. I used to be able to turn a single rejection into months of grieving and self-hatred and resentment where I excused myself from trying to do anything else. Looking back, I feel sad for that young woman I put through so much pain. I had no idea that it was totally unnecessary to live that way. The most amazing thing is that most of the time, when I get through one of these episodes, I come out feeling better on the other side. This kind of emotional growth, that is almost all but impossible for the practicing alcoholic, makes life an adventure worth living that never in my wildest imagination when I was imprisoned in the drinking life, could I have believed was possible. And all I had to do to set this change in motion was to stop drinking, one day at a time.

I've been to AA meetings all over the world – in Cambodia, France, Belgium, England, Wales, in the Arctic, in bomb shelters in Israel, in the Navajo Nation, on military bases in Kabul, all over the United States and Canada. Instead of finding "companions" in bars, I meet sober alcoholics in meetings. We don't have to explain to each other why we don't drink, or why want to stop drinking. We know why. We only want to know how – because we've all been in the same place, we've all experienced the profound, painful, insatiable and horrific psychic and physical emptiness of alcoholism. No one who has escaped it wants to go back. The great solution that rehab and AA presented to me was that there was one other thing that could relieve my craving: talking about it with other alcoholics who shared my desire to stop drinking.

Today, I can't imagine wanting a drink anymore than I used to not be able to imagine not wanting a drink. The foundation of my recovery, my happiness, and everything and everyone that matters to me is built on what I was given in rehab and AA: mutual understanding and support.

25. An Activist in Sobriety

John L.

Some alcoholics are born that way – periodic drunks, who can stay away from a drink for a long time, but for whom a first drink always means disaster. Others, daily drinkers, acquire alcoholism; they drink too much over time until they cross the invisible line.

I was a bit of both – but alcohol alone did not make me an alcoholic. Shame and self-hatred, from living as a gay man in a malevolent culture, took their toll. I didn't just drink to relax inhibitions or to escape; I drank to kill myself.

My parents were social drinkers. My father believed that men became alcoholics because they didn't know how to drink – implicitly, that they couldn't drink like gentlemen. As a child I was occasionally allowed to taste wine if it was served with dinner.

I had my first drink when I was about eight. My father's best friend (later to die from alcoholism) had a birthday party. Stuck into the birthday cake, instead of candles, were little glasses filled with *Creme de Menthe*. The other kids just tasted it and made faces, but I drank a whole glass.

I was born in a small town in the midwest, a few years before World War II. My early childhood memories are dark, an atmosphere of imminent doom. My father and the fathers of most of my friends were overseas; we didn't know if they would ever return, and some of them didn't. There were rationing, blackout air raid drills, and omnipresent propaganda. There was always fear.

My adolescence was in the 1950s of the McCarthy era, which ushered in another kind of fear, the fear of being different. Nonconformity amounted to treason. As gay men were purged from employment, branded as traitors, vilified in the yellow press, and driven to suicide, my awakening sexuality was informed by terror. It was to be sealed off, neither discussed nor acted upon.

It could have been worse. I had good friends and teachers, was on the track and debate teams, and was active as a pianist. Without much effort, I always made the honor roll. In high school we had "beer blasts" – went out to the river in the country with cases of beer. I drank as much as anyone, but never became drunk, and I always drove home.

My National Merit and College Board scores put me in the top 0.1 percentile of college-bound seniors, so I was accepted by every college I applied to, as well as several I hadn't. I chose Harvard. On the very first day, the proctor of my freshman dorm introduced himself and served us sherry, which greatly impressed me. Although legally underage, I had no trouble buying wine or beer, which I drank in moderation.

In my freshman year I was allowed to take advanced courses, which were usually open only to upperclassmen. This was difficult, but at the end of the year I had almost made the Dean's List. Then disaster struck on the very last day: my first bender.

Two friends and I had been drinking, just a few beers. Then something happened which upset me. With a sure instinct I opened a fifth of scotch, intended for my father the next day, and I chug-a-lugged it.

I'm not sure "bender" is the right word, but I can't think of a better one. I mean drinking almost to the point of death, with horrible physical aftereffects. Alcohol can kill in a hundred ways, and this is one. Every year, young men die in fraternity hazings, when they are forced to drink more than their bodies can handle.

That first bender was truly horrible. I had a splitting headache, shook violently, and had wet and dry heaves: I'd vomit thick, bitter, yellow stuff, and when no more came up, I'd have spasms. Then I'd drink water and more would come up. For weeks I couldn't even think about alcohol without nausea. But in time I returned to the dog that bit me.

I did manage to graduate from college, but just barely. Alcohol bombed my academic prospects. After graduation I moved to New York City, where, after some false starts, I started a career in market research.

I drank alcoholically for ten years – from that first bender when I was 18 to my last drink when I was 28. I crossed the "invisible line" early on, in terms of blackouts, hangovers, and disasters in my personal life. But, like many alcoholics, I deluded myself.

Much of my drinking took place in gay bars, which were the only places where gay men could safely meet each other. Alcohol, which dissolved shame and inhibitions, became inseparable from sex and socialising.

For a decade I drank daily, mostly as a moderate to heavy social drinker. For long periods of time – for months or even a year once – I could drink like this. However, periodically, with no warning whatever, I would lose control, and then anything could happen. Some very bad things happened to me in this decade, and I did bad things myself, but I was by no means always drunk, and there were some beautiful moments also.

In the 1960s, the Lower East Side of New York City was the center of "The Movement" – counterculturists and radicals of all kinds. My friends and I were involved in underground publications, radical politics, art, and theater. I'm proud that from 1965 on I was part of the movement to stop the war in Vietnam. I was only a foot soldier, but I did what I could. Much of my drinking took place in Stanley's bar on East 12th Street and Avenue B and in the Old Reliable bar on East 3rd Street. These bars were famous in the underground, and people from all over the world came to drink in them. What conversations we had! I wish I could remember a few. Many times I drank and talked until closing time at three or four in the morning. These were not gay bars, but if I wanted a bedfellow for the night, I usually found one.

Alcohol was my best friend and my deadliest enemy. My shyness went away when I drank. I made love to many guys (each time committing a felony by the laws of the time). But it got worse, and the enemy began to take over.

After one traumatic episode, hungover and suicidal, I found myself in a hospital emergency room. A young intern explained alcoholism to me and suggested I try AA. My immediate response was that I didn't need religious nuts. He countered by saying that many AA members are not religious. I didn't listen. Another couple of alcoholic years lay before me.

In the last year of so of my drinking I became isolated, drinking more and more by myself in my apartment on St. Mark's Place. My tolerance fell, so that even a small amount of alcohol would upset me, at the same time that I could no longer get drunk. My health collapsed. I almost died in end-stage alcohol withdrawal: delirium tremens (DTs) and an alcoholic convulsion.

In my delirium I had an epiphany: the realisation that I was dying from hatred – hatred from within myself and hatred from outside – hatred caused by guilt and shame over being gay in a hateful culture. At the same time I felt a sudden and intense desire to live, a determination to defy the culture that hated me. These insights would inform the course of my recovery.

My friend Andy found me and saved my life. He explained AA and took me to my first meeting – Perry Street Workshop in early January of 1968. After a brief slip, I had my last drink in February of 1968. For several weeks I was still sick and close to death, but with treatment from Dr. Frank Seixas, a top alcoholism specialist, I made a good physical recovery.

I've told the story of my physical recovery and my early AA experiences in my book, *A Freethinker in Alcoholics Anonymous*, so I'll be brief here. I attended mostly Greenwich Village meetings or the Midnight meeting in Chelsea. After achieving a year of sobriety, I gave my first "qualification" (talk) and started speaking at meetings all over Manhattan. I spoke at a meeting in the Upper East Side, where, it was rumored, most of the members were in the Social Register. I spoke at Sober Sams on the Bowery, before about 200 homeless men in the Salvation Army shelter. I felt at home in both groups. I truly believe that AA in those days was more intense, and had less religiosity, than now. No matter how different the groups were, they all emphasised staying away from the First Drink a day at a time.

As a low-bottom drunk physically, I have never doubted that my life depends on total abstinence. Picking up the First Drink would be signing my death warrant. Although AA is only a small part of my life, my AA sobriety is first priority.

Much of my life has been devoted to causes of one kind or another. In June 1969, after I had been sober for a year and a half, the Stonewall Riots took place in Greenwich Village, a half mile from my apartment. This led to the birth of Gay Liberation, the movement I had always been waiting for, and I jumped in. Since then my life has been largely devoted to this cause, the emancipation of male love – to destroy the theological taboo on sex between males and to restore male love (comprising love, friendship and sex) to a place of honor in society, as in Ancient Greece. I have organised marches and picket lines, given speeches, and written books and articles. But this is another story.

Besides the antiwar and Gay Liberation movements, I've been a prominent critic of "AIDS" orthodoxy, and have written about English Romantics, the men in the Shelley-Byron circle, maintaining heretically that there is much homoeroticism in their lives and works and that Percy Bysshe Shelley himself, rather than his second wife, Mary, is the author of *Frankenstein*. For all this, I've received my share of bouquets and brickbats.

I consider myself engaged in a struggle against superstition, not only in the area of sexuality, but also that of recovery. I'm proud to be part of the rapidly growing movement to secularise AA – to strengthen the True AA, the AA of the 24-Hour Plan and the Fellowship, and to weaken the False AA of dogmatism, cultic behavior, conformity, intolerance, anti-intellectualism, and helpless-without-God religiosity.

I've attended AA meetings throughout the United States and much of the world. Almost always I've felt the strengthening power of the Fellowship. I've usually managed to find groups with a maximum of fellowship and a minimum of religiosity. My preference is for small, closed discussion meetings, rather than meetings open to the general public. I also prefer men's meetings to mixed meetings, believing that there is greater candour and intimacy, and less religiosity, in the former.

Looking to the future, I intend to bear witness as an open non-believer in AA with long-term sobriety. I want the newcomer to know that the Steps and almost everything in the first 164 pages of the Big Book are optional. There is really just one essential: Don't pick up the First Drink! I don't go looking for fights, but am not afraid to rebuke an aggressive Big-Book-thumper. Often, when I have done this, others have supported me. But whether I am supported or alone, I will be true to myself and true to AA as it ought to be.

Sobriety should mean reclaiming our intelligence, not dumbing it down – living the one life we have to the fullest.

26. A Holy Terror of an Alcoholic

Cheryl K.

A short-lived, yet holy terror of an alcoholic ride commenced when I was arrested, handcuffed, and escorted from High School on charges of possession with intent to distribute. I was fifteen years old.

By my senior year, I was hospitalized for breaking my head open when I ran through a red light, hit a police car, and totaled the car I was driving – I was in a blackout and remember nothing of it. These occurrences failed to signal a need to stop drinking and drugging. In the alcoholic home I lived in, these instances were not considered outrageous. Everything was someone else's fault in our alcoholic world. One morning I was backing out of our driveway when I heard and felt a big thwack. I had taken the door off a repair truck parked in front of the neighbor's house. I stopped just long enough to give Dad's number to the repairman. That was how I operated. That was all. If I sound uncaring, I really was. If I sound blasé about my legal troubles, it is because my alcoholic father was not only my primary enabler he was also my attorney.

My parents were divorced and I lived with my Mom until the afore-mentioned arrest at age fifteen. I called my Dad from the jail and he appeared in short order with an arsenal of rhetorical tools that he employed to satisfy the police and inform me that what was needed was a geographic cure. I was to move to his house where he could keep an eye on me. I was skeptical but relieved.

My Dad's house had an open bar and there was no one to monitor my comings and goings. I dreaded telling Mom, but Dad took me to see her that afternoon and we told her the plan. Her soft brown eyes revealed the tragedy of a mother losing her youngest child and even more than that, they showed the fear of impending tragedies to come as she imagined all that could and would go wrong allowing a fifteen-year-old girl to live in a home without limits or supervision.

Moving to Dad's meant a new school and new friends. The first day of class, I befriended a fellow alcoholic who would be pivotal in my drinking and my sobriety. My new friend had a Dad who lived out of town but supplied unlimited funds that assured our next two years were filled with outrageous alcoholic benders.

In our senior year, my friend began seeing a therapist who suggested she go to AA. She did. And then she dragged my sister to AA with her. I was horrified at this turn of events. But they began to change in a way that even I could see was good. I consented to go with them to an AA meeting. What I found were familiar faces: friends I hadn't seen in the last year or so. Everyone was happy and laughing even as they talked about the struggle to be young and sober. They were living ways that they felt good about. I knew immediately that I was somewhere I wanted to be. I moved back to Mom's the next day while Dad was at work; my sister stayed sober and she moved back to Mom's as well.

For the next fourteen years I lived a sober life; my sister was sober for most of this time as well. These were good years. I worked the steps of AA and became part of the fellowship. I learned how to live, how to recognize and amend those things I had done that made me feel ashamed. I learned how to express my gratitude through action, and how to feel really good about myself through contributing my unique talents to the world. I fell in love, went to University and began living a life that was happy, joyous, and free.

It was during my stint at University – majoring in Religious Studies – that I became aware of my atheism. Atheism was not something I sought, it simply happened. I grieved the loss of the god of my understanding. I was scared, but eventually I realized that my atheism was just a new part of my truth. I stayed sober and continued to work the steps utilizing the universe for the god of my understanding. I did curb my meeting attendance because I grew weary of making my ideas fit into the a quasi-Abrahamic god that was talked about at AA: the god that kept deserving alcoholics sober, saved parking spots for the good folks of AA, and turned agnostics into believers according to Chapter Four of the Big Book. This god was increasingly at odds with my own way of thinking, and eventually I quit attending meetings altogether.

My best friend from High School became my romantic life partner after a few years of sobriety. We drank together, got sober together, and after college we opened a business together. We employed our friends – sober alcoholics – and our business flourished. Since I had quit going to meetings, my connection to AA was strictly through work, my primary relationship, and our best friends, my sister and her husband who were both sober. My sister had given birth to my beautiful nephew and we all spent countless hours of joy with this tiny wonder. His first years of life were sweet times for the four of us. We were young, sober, hardworking, and successful.

In 1995 I turned 30; this would prove a watershed year for me. My ten-year primary relationship came to an end. It was amicable and so very sad. We sold our business, and our friends and family were split apart. This same year, my sister and her husband divorced and my sister began drinking. By the start of 1996, my ties to AA were almost non-existent. I was terribly lonely. I began dating and found myself around drinking for the first time as an adult. Still, I never considered having a drink; I never considered going to a meeting either.

I did think to take a geographic cure to Thailand in hopes that halfway around the world I would escape my loneliness. I was traveling alone and began spending my days with a small group of fellow travelers from England. We met each afternoon for tea and one day someone ordered champagne at our afternoon gathering. To be polite, I decided to pick up the bubbly drink and sip. I drank two or three glasses, was told I was "pissed," and set off for a nap. I did not drink again. There was no craving. It had been wonderful and ladylike and I was fine. Moreover, I now knew what I had suspected for quite some time... I was not an alcoholic. I completely dismissed my High School drinking as normal adolescent experimentation. Besides, AA had taught me that one drink would set up a sort of mad craving for unlimited quantities of alcohol that would end with me penniless, toothless, and rolling in the gutter. Nothing of the sort happened. In fact, I had my next drink many months later. Again, I was on vacation, a perfectly acceptable time and place to have a drink. I ordered a glass of wine with my dinner and drank it. Voilà. Cured. Let the drinking begin! And it was fun and I drank politely... for about one hot minute.

Consistent drinking began in 1997 with civilized Tuesday afternoon cocktails at poolside – I had a lovely home with a perfect, princess swimming pool. My drinking ended with me living in a tiny, broken-down apartment, financially propped up with student loans and the overburdened assistance of my family and friends. By the time I quit drinking in 2007, I had less than nothing. I was emaciated, wrinkled, addle-brained, and in serious debt – aka penniless, toothless, and rolling in the gutter.

I had managed during the early days of my drinking to return to school, having earned an academic scholarship for a Master's degree. Somehow, I completed the Master's program and I was awarded a Teaching Fellowship, which I felt was a real hardship considering the hours required to study, attend class, and practice my alcoholism. I never once felt grateful or thought of the obligation I had to give back to the University that was bankrolling me. I had reverted to my former alcoholic outlook where everything was someone else's fault and responsibility. I received an undeserved reward with this opportunity to teach, but I fell in love with my students, and teaching helped me keep one toe on the planet as I continued to drink my way through the days ahead.

I graduated and began the Doctoral program because I didn't know anything else I could actually do and continue with my drinking career. The delightful experience of my company justified anyone and everyone footing the bill for me. I was far too ashamed to allow myself to recognize that I was a parasite on society, my family, and friends. I pretended that the generosity I received was normal, that my lack of finances was temporary and would be resolved when I finished my Doctoral program. But somewhere I knew that I could never finish my degree because I had no idea what I was doing. I did well in my classes because I obsessed and worked like a madman between my drunken bouts. But there was no way for me to corral my thoughts into a cohesive dissertation. I just kept taking classes and hanging on by a thread.

In 2006 my precious nephew, my sister's son, was drinking and drugging and some serious consequences were unfolding for him at his High School. My sister was normalizing his addictive behavior and even drinking with him in order to remain in denial about her own problem. I grew frantic for his well being and I decided to quit drinking in order to help him. I failed. I called my on-again off-again girlfriend of many years to save me. She came and committed to helping my nephew in any way she could, but she did not want to resume her relationship with me. She had been there for me through everything and she had seen me at my alcoholic worst – sloppy, ugly, dishonest, entitled, crazy-eyed, blacked out, dirty, degenerate, and desperate. She had never turned me away, no matter how badly I had behaved and she was one of the only people in my life who knew me when I was a more decent version of myself: sober.

But she had finally had enough of my chaos. She was going to NA and she was happy. I went home to my ramshackle apartment. I had never felt so alone. I made a decision to get sober. I mean by this that I took Step One of Alcoholics Anonymous. Even in the very first instant of taking this step, I felt relief. I searched my book-shelves and found a copy of the Big Book. There was a great deal of the old concept of god in there, but I didn't care. That was May 18, 2007. I got sober that night and I have remained sober since.

Some people believe that you can't get sober without a god, without going to meetings, and without getting a sponsor. I did get sober, and without any of those things. What I did do was change my habits and work a modified (god-less) version of the steps that made sense to me. At first, I just meditated and made art. I painted, wrote poetry, made videos, designed and sewed clothing, anything at all. And I called my Mom. My precious Mom who never gave up on me. Mom took me to the doctor and encouraged me to eat. She stayed with me in my tiny apartment. We laughed and cried and she guided me back to the land of the living.

When I am drinking and drugging, I am tormented; I think this is true for all addicts. Not consciously tormented, but it's always there, just below the surface. The program of AA can help us to alleviate the drinking long enough to clear up some of the wreckage, forgive ourselves, and return to lives filled with joy and peace. It is possible and even probable with a bit of effort.

Today I am happily married, gainfully employed (teaching!), and my nephew has been sober for almost eight years. I remain acutely aware of the ease with which I found a drink in my hand. Endeav-oring to maintain my sobriety, I attend meetings at a We Agnostics, Atheists, and Free Thinkers (WAAFT) AA group recently estab-lished in my own neighborhood. We are a group, like all AA groups, that finds the fellowship assists us in achieving our common goals: to stay sober and help other alcoholics to achieve sobriety.

27. My Alcohol-Addicted Agnostic-Atheist Recovery Story

Thomas B.

Hello, I'm Thomas B. and I'm primarily addicted to the liquid legal drug, ethanol, preferably Colt .45 – by the case lot, daily. However presently I'm in my forty-third year of ongoing recovery, a day at a time. My spiritual progress has been that I came into AA fearful of going to hell, but this has morphed over the last several years into an agnostic atheism with Buddhist/Hindu leanings and a smattering of lots of New Agey stuff. I meditate daily and still pray, at times somewhat frantically, not for divine intervention, but in an attempt to quell my sometimes raucously racing mind. An agnostic-atheist? Yup, I don't believe there is a God, but I also can't know for sure that there is not!

But, I get ahead of myself. Let me tell you how it was.

What It Was Like

I grew up in a middle-class, white collar family in Jackson, MS, from prominent southern Baptist and Presbyterian Scotch-Norman clans. Mother got religion and converted to Catholicism when I was in the throes of puberty. I tagged along because my best friend was Catholic, and I wanted to drink, smoke, gamble and dance without the terror of everlasting hell.

My first girlfriend at the time, Judy, a non-practicing Baptist, with whom I had won a jitter-bug contest at Arthur Murray, promptly ditched me because I worshipped an idol of the Virgin Mary. I didn't realize that to even think about masturbation as a Catholic, much less to do it, would damn me to hell forever and ever and ever were I to be struck dead before I could confess and receive absolution from a priest.

About the same time, age 12 or 13, I started drinking. One of my first horrid drunks was camping with a couple of buddies and getting hammered on stolen altar wine.

I was never a social drinker and never became the cool, slick, debonair chick-magnet, life-of-the-party kind of guy. Whenever I drank, even several beers, my speech became slurred. Most of the time, I got sloppily drunk and this included occasionally throwing up on a date, a decided impediment to getting a walk to first base, much less hitting a grand slammer. Whenever I drank, what early-on I judged to be an unmanageable life became utterly unbearable!

Now, mind you, externally my life was peachy keen. Good grades, lots of friends, starting football player, a star even sometimes, leading man in theatre productions, a different one-and-one-only-forever sweetheart each year of high school, president of my senior class.

Didn't matter. Internally I was a fearful, nervous, isolated, alienated, teenybopper – no pimples or acme, but with a huge inferiority complex not soothed by any ego-enhancing achievements. I looked in the mirror and saw a gawky, gangly, geeky misfit. I was only faking it, somehow getting by, and if only my classmates knew the real me, I would be forever spurned and shunned.

This state of "incomprehensible demoralization" continued throughout four years of college at Xavier University in Cincinnati, where under the tutelage of Jesuits I became an agnostic. I continued doing well in studies, graduating with honors. I was also heavily involved in extra-curricular activities, producing and starring in most theatre productions, elected to student government, an editor of the newspaper, etc.

However, my most important activity was the two to four hours every night I spent drinking, usually by myself, in a lowdown bar, as far across the railroad tracks as one could get. There in a darkened corner with pitchers of 3.2% beer, I would carefully watch the old geezers come in, shaking and downing that desperately needed first shot followed by a beer chaser. I was convinced then that they were what I was destined to become.

So why did I drink? Because I was addicted, because it was the only thing I could do to get a few moments of relief or, better yet, to pass out. Because I could literally cry in my beer and feel some-thing, even if it were awful. I was much more terrified of feeling nothing, being a numb automaton, a no man. I preferred being a bad drunk rather than a no man.

By the time I flunked out of my first year of grad school at Xavier, shortly after another relationship ended, I was convinced there was no way I could ever get satisfaction – as the Stones famously sang

– much less love and happiness, since I was such a loser. I became increasingly suicidal in thought, just wanting IT, my life, to end.

However, I was petrified of putting a bullet in my head or driving a car into a tree at high speed out of terror that some god, despite doubting one even existed, would manifest itself out of the Kosmos and send me to hell forever. So, I volunteered to go to Vietnam in 1967 and 1968, so Charlie would do what I was too chicken-shit to do.

Didn't work. Despite my best efforts during a time of ever-mounting American KIA casualties, even though I volunteered for every extra-hazardous duty assignment I could, I somehow survived despite myself to come home to a ready-made family, having gotten married two days before I flew to Vietnam to my casual girl-friend at the time, who was pregnant with our first daughter.

The next several years were spent finishing my active duty army commitment, going to graduate school for theatre, which I also flunked out of because I was too drunk to pass the oral exams, and getting my wife pregnant with our second daughter, while having an affair with my real one and true only love. Most important, I got drunk every day and obsessively still fantasized about suicide. Unmanageable? You betcha!

After convincing my real true love to be named co-respondent, providing love letters between us as evidence of my unfaithfulness for a quick and dirty divorce from wife No. 1, I moved to New York City to pursue a career in the theatre and married wife No. 2.

What Happened

In a story I shared on AA Agnostica, "First AA Meetings", I detail how this second marriage became the impetus for me to get into recovery in October of 1972 at age 29. Through the human power of the AA Fellowship, I've been sober ever since.

I am forever grateful that I found recovery in New York City where the formula for staying sober was "Don't Drink, Go to Meetings, Help Others". I threw myself into service at the group level and co-chaired the first New York City Young People's AA Conference. I was also able to finish – finally! – a third graduate school, Columbia University, with a masters in psychiatric social work and enjoyed a successful thirty year career in the field of addiction treatment.

Early in my second year of recovery I got a sponsor, Peter, who guided me for 33 years. Our friendship deepened when we shared an AA sober house on Fire Island for several summers. It was with Peter that I started meditating. My first time meditating I had a mind-blowing, white-light experience as powerful as any account I've read of what can happen under the influence of psychedelics.

We spent hours discussing our various spiritual pursuits. These included attending numerous workshops and weekend retreats, with voluminous readings in the world's spiritual traditions, astrology, rebirthing, yoga, New Thought, and several New Age gurus and authors which included Ram Dass and Alan Watts. During the 80s, we also became heavily involved with "A Course in Miracles". Yup, we were prime examples of our woo-woo baby-boomer generation!

I married for a third time in 1980, and we had a son, who shares recovery with me. One of the most spiritual moments of my recovery was witnessing his birth. Especially since my first daughter was born when I was in Vietnam, and I was royally hammered when my second daughter was born in 1971. That marriage also destroyed itself on the shoals of passing time in 2001. While awaiting the sale of our Victorian cottage on the South Shore of Long Island to close, I spent a couple of weeks down at ground zero following 911 in Lower Manhattan as a Red Cross Mental Health Volunteer with first responders.

One of the most desperate years of my life was going on the road in a Rialta RV bought with my half of the proceeds from selling our home. In anguish, I did what I have always done since 1972 – I didn't drink, and I went to meetings all over the U.S. and Canada, prior to settling down for a couple of years in Tucson, Arizona.

In 2003, disgusted as a Vietnam Vet that we were doing it again, invading another far-off foreign country, Iraq, I expatriated for two years to Sri Lanka, serving as an unarmed peacekeeper between the Buddhist Sinhalese Army and the minority Hindu Tamil Tigers. I used the Grapevine and monthly meetings in Colombo to do what I've done since 1972, stay sober a day at a time.

I also survived the devastating Tsunami the morning of December 26, 2004. About 15 minutes before the 30-foot high wave demolished the guest house complex where I was staying, I left the grounds on the pristine beach of the Bay of Bengal near Trincomalee to go on a bike ride inland to visit a 2,200 year old Buddhist/Hindu/Vedda Temple complex deep in the jungle. Providence? I think not – just another example of my Scotch-Norman luck.

After Sri Lanka, I moved back to New York, meeting and marrying my fourth wife, Jill, also in longterm recovery, whom I met at an ACA meeting. In 2011, we decided to relocate to a small town, Coos Bay, on the southern coast of Oregon. To say we experienced a culture shock is a vast understatement. AA was primarily oriented to a strict parsing of the Big Book, which they haughtily profess is just a tad smaller than their Biggest Book, the Bible. There, we experienced AA as a fundamentalist Christian cult!

What It's Like Now

In the same way that I am grateful to have found recovery in New York City in 1972, so, too, am I most grateful for stumbling across the AA Agnostica website in early 2012. Who knows? Had I not connected with AA Agnostica, I very well might have drunk again, so alienated was I from the small-town, Christian fundamentalist prejudice my wife and I experienced in Coos freaking Bay. We were not only shunned, we were also shamed for our non-traditional beliefs. Thankfully, we were able to move to another seacoast town, Seaside, which is a reasonable commute to Portland where we started a Beyond Belief meeting on December 1, 2013.

I was mortified to experience my first and only "Back to Basics" meeting in Frederick, MD, while Jill and I were visiting my daughters and grandchildren. Our experience in Coos Bay and connection with AA Agnostica with its numerous agnostic-atheist friendly articles has made me realize how fortunate I've been for most of my recovery to experience AA in New York. I was mostly oblivious to how radically AA has been changing over the past several decades. It has become increasingly more doctrinaire, largely focused upon an evangelical and pietistic Christian focus on the Big Book.

Even in Portland, Oregon, one of the most progressive cities in North America, the program is increasingly God-centered. All meetings ritualistically read "How It Works" and announce that only AA conference-approved literature can be used in meetings. Indeed, some groups are lobbying for the Portland Intergroup Office to only sell conference-approved literature.

Nevertheless, my intention is to remain a member of AA until I pass into whatever lies beyond this mortal coil. In the meantime, I shall continue to not drink and go to meetings, where I share my non-religious experience, strength and hope.

I am ever so grateful to be engaged with other agnostics, atheists and freethinkers in our expanding movement within the AA Fellowship. We help each other not only to stay sober, but we also encourage ourselves to tell the truth of our human power to recover, as AA members who deeply doubt or are without belief in the intervention of any alleged deity. The growth of our meetings around the world and the inspiring experience many of us shared in Santa Monica provide me with great gratitude and awe-inspiring hope!

28. Embracing Our Pain Together

By Alyssa S.

I'm sitting here reflecting upon the day of St. Valentine. It is bitterly cold outside.

It's time in my recovery for "me time" – a time for introspection, perhaps for self-love.

I have longed for this for many years. Despite the pain and fear I've already encountered, I have faith in love through sobriety. I am at a place where I recognize the denial of my behaviour which has direct correlation to my alcoholism. I haven't confronted this type of clarity until now. I've certainly never experienced this kind of self awareness.

In a broader sense I am embracing empathy and compassion for the human race at a depth of enlightenment that I've never experienced. Of course, with any new expansion within the human psyche, parallel experiences will begin to surface, causing some to feel connected. As a newcomer, hypersensitivity is prominent in my journey today. One could compare the excitement to a child first tasting ice cream, or the pain from an undesired consequence. Recognizing commonalities in phases of sobriety is helpful and engaging for me. This is partly why I'm drawn to old-timer wisdom. They've been there and done that – although not all old-timers' have wisdom. I'm learning to draw conclusions about people with whom I want relationships, while learning boundaries through assessing my own behavior.

I grew up with parents who worked in social services, addictions and family therapy. Naturally, part of my mission would be to follow in the footsteps of my role models. Alcohol was never a factor in my childhood, and my surroundings were free of addictions. My mother's career was in social services and my father was a psychotherapist and social worker. He was an addictions specialist within the ARF (Addictions Research Foundation), before they amalgamated into CAMH (Centre for Addictions and Mental Health) in Toronto. He was involved in creating a link between treatment centres and AA. He was the founder of recovery homes and trained many psychiatrists using the therapeutic techniques that assisted thousands of people. Before learning he was Métis

Cree, he was drawn toward training within First Nation's communities. I loved him and when he passed away three and half years ago, it not only broke my heart, but built me up.

The goal of my parents was to raise an emotionally healthy child, while providing a foundation of safety for free expression and assertive communication. A girl who thinks and reasons for herself is the meaning of my name, Alyssa. Throughout my life and drinking career, I would learn that if I abandoned my truth, I would suffer greatly, more than any other loss would ever generate.

There was no drinking around me as a child. My parents were child centred in that decade of their lives. I believe that the nature versus nurture argument is inclusive to both explanations. I believe genetics and environmental factors both contribute toward the development of alcoholism. Genetics played a role in my life because I picked up before I ever saw alcohol in my environment at age 11.

Rum, Gin, Rye, Triple Sec, Tequila, Kahlua, and the list goes on. The bartender's guide to get your teenager as drunk as possible in a safe environment. All these liquors, I would acquire at very early age, and I had a bar in my bedroom by the age of 16. Hey, the party was on my porch. There were enablers in my life and people I could manipulate. Suddenly, this child centred home, full of love and tolerance, would crumble and turn into an alcohol focused environment. Healthy brain development as a youth became distorted by alcohol abuse, which compromised my self-image and led me to present myself as a seductive teenage girl. Smoking rainbow cigarettes in jazz bars and pretending I was older, I learned to compartmentalize my experiences in a way I felt safe. Numbing my reality kept me away from experiencing unpleasant emotions. I was a pot head by day and a drinker by noon.

My father, an expert in the field of addictions, tried to keep me safe inside the walls of the house. I know he was terrified to think that his daughter had turned into his worst nightmare. I think it's a huge topic that faces the parents of teenage alcoholics. What is enabling? How much is too much? Should I put her in a group home and operate through tough love? It must be torment for a parent with a similar affliction.

And then, he relapsed himself, after 40 years of sobriety. Just like that, depression and lack of any supportive agnostic environment took its toll.

We all began drinking under the same roof. My mother drank her wine, I drank my liquor and my father drank his fantasy concoction of soda, grape juice and alcohol, and convinced himself it was helping his stomach, while remaining in the dark about a painful relapse. He suffered from numerous health problems. Nobody communicated their pain and fear anymore. Family meetings turned into threats, crying and manipulation. And back to drinking again. We all suffered.

I'm eternally grateful there was love in my foundation. I was terrified of being abandoned. Out of the many things I learned from this man, the most important was to have faith in love and forgiveness. He hit a gold mine when learning to manipulate me based on fear. He fabricated stories about finding a teenage girl on drugs, who was stuck in a mental episode for the rest of her life. He knew my fear of going crazy would stop me from doing hard drugs like ecstasy, special K, and Crystal Meth. This method worked. Alcohol and marijuana became my escape.

Embracing our pain together, as my Dad would die from the crippling disease of Parkinson's, has saved me today. He was sober again and so was I. We were stronger when we could support each other.

It's all a learning experience and insight into who I am today. That's what my therapist told me recently. This was probably to get me to operate by solution focus and quit harbouring shame and guilt from the past. Can you tell I'm pro therapy? My Dad once said, in my early sobriety, before my 2 year relapse and after his relapse, "you need to get your own therapist again." I think he wanted me to build my own foundation. I love therapy. It's a relationship between two people and you have the opportunity to analyze everything. If you're a family therapist, which is something I aspire to be eventually, you get to analyze more.

The work I would go on to pursue, is a huge part of who I am. In high school, I began to study female genital mutilation and childhood sexual abuse. I think I scared the shit out of some of my peers, unintentionally. I was so drawn to learning about childhood sexual abuse and other childhood traumas because my Dad was a victim and I saw the mental health issues that arose from this horrific experience. I developed immense respect for survivors and an empathic understanding. I experienced rage and anger on behalf of the survivor in my early studies.

I went onto college to complete my child and youth diploma and spend the next 10 years as a child therapist in group homes and the school board, drinking and relapsing all the way through. Summers became a blur of alcohol poisoning and threats of being kicked out of my boyfriend's house.

I would manipulate my way back through the charm and charisma that I developed in my early 20s. Brad was my first love. He was killed through an act of violence at 24 and I was only 23 years old. I had just finished college with honours. He was so proud of me. He was an artist and a brilliant young man. He was a believer in the spirit world and he and I would often debate within my limited perspective. It was debating for the sake of debating and to evaluate how much control you have over the other person's emotions.

After Brad's passing, I drank 24/7, had multiple partners, encouraged a young woman to develop a business in the sex trade, and hosted chaos everywhere I went. I'm ashamed of my behaviour when I look back and examine. I continue working through these painful emotions today. My high risk behaviour led me into situations where rape and crisis occurred more times than I can count on one hand. Escaping from being held captive by a rapist only kept me off the bottle for one month. When I drank again, my whole head caught on fire from a candle. Car accidents and chronic back problems are part of my shame. My rock bottom was a series of events and I manipulated my way out of being charged four more times. I gave the police a pity story every time. An ability which many alcoholics possess.

Sitting here on Valentine's Day for the first time single in over a decade, I realize that I have given up my old playmates, play places and playthings. This is born of wisdom that my brother has shown me. He is an old-timer now with decades of sobriety and he understands the darkness of relapse. He has the exact wisdom I need at this time and I ask for it. We have the same blood and although he is decades older, It feels good knowing he's connected to me.

Today, as an alcoholic, I have a second home. It is Alcoholics Anonymous. I always felt excluded from AA because I needed to get beyond the God focused language and couldn't. Jim B. "A god of my understanding."

But now I've finally developed a relationship with AA. Now, I can go into any room and be okay to hear your story. It's because I've built a bond with others who feel excluded from AA and rejected by Intergroup. My family is a group of non believers, agnostics, free thinkers and, some religious people who believe solely in discussing recovery options. These people – who embrace me and hold my hands even though I don't accept the "God bit" – are my anchor. In May of 2011, the Greater Toronto Area (GTA) Intergroup rejected two agnostic groups and kicked them off of the official AA meeting list. What intergroup did is keeping out the vast majority of young non-believers. We hide in the hallway. AA needs to open the doors. This is your chance AA, to open your heart to all alcoholics and blossom with the future.

Knock, knock. I want back in. It's Valentine's Day. And it's bitterly cold outside.

29. Take What You Need and Leave the Rest

Chuck K.

I sobered up in the Care Unit at St. Elizabeth Hospital on Chicago's northwest side in June, 1982. Members of AA from the Logan Square Alano Club chaired three meetings a week in the ward room.

They emphasized three things – the cunning, baffling power of booze, the greater power of God, and the 12 Steps of Alcoholics Anonymous. They stated they were powerless over alcohol and I nodded with understanding. I was powerless too. They told me to go to daily meetings when I got out of rehab and that seemed to be a good idea. They told me to work the 12 steps of the program and get a sponsor to help me do that. That also seemed like a reasonable thing to do. Finally they told me to get down on my knees and pray to God for help or I'd get drunk again.

That was a problem. I'd been an atheist since I was twenty. Now nineteen years later, people were telling me to go to God. I thought it was a waste of time but I didn't want to start drinking again, realized there were things I didn't know, and decided to follow directions for a change.

After the meeting where I'd been told to pray, I took the elevator to the chapel on the eleventh floor. The only light was the candle burning next to the tabernacle on the altar. I knelt down in the aisle and stared at the candle, waiting for something to transpire, for some change in my heart. Nothing happened so I cleared my throat and said, "If you're there and you have something to tell me, I'm listening."

The room was silent. The candle flickered but nothing else happened. That's when I realized my sobriety was in my own hands, not God's or anyone else's. I got up a changed person. I'd bent my will to the wisdom of the program and despite my misgivings, done something I considered foolish because I was truly over alcohol and willing to go to any lengths to get sober.

I went back to my room, relieved that I wouldn't have to become a holy roller to maintain my new-found sobriety, and looked through a

Chicago meeting directory. I searched for meetings to attend once I was released from the Care Unit. I was dismayed to find most met in churches and seemed religious in focus, such as the Thursday Night Meditation Group, the Miracles Happen Group, the Came to Believe Group, and the Resurrection Group.

I complained about the seeming religious bent of the program to my counselor who shrugged and said, "It's not so bad. Lots of people who think like you change their tune about God and come around in a few months. You know what it says in the Big Book in the chapter 'We Agnostics', right?"

"Yeah, patronizing and highly insulting," I answered.

"Well, there's an atheist and agnostic meeting on Mondays at the Second Unitarian Church. That's Don W.'s meeting. You might like that. Tell him I said hello if you stop by."

"I will," I said, "thanks for the information."

I left the hospital on Friday. Monday night I attended my first Quad A meeting.

I arrived at the church with a bit of trepidation and went downstairs to the basement where the meeting was taking place next to the furnace and the janitor's utility sink. The room was filled with loud, raucous conversation and sounded like a late-night barroom. I got a cup of coffee and sat down at the back of room, careful to avoid the low-hanging steam pipes.

Smoke billowed across the tables (people still smoked at meetings in those days) and it didn't take me long to figure out this was not a typical AA meeting where the recovering inebriates let go and let God. Here the members of the fellowship cursed profusely, labeled Ronald Reagan a fascist reactionary, and denounced religion as a delusional disease. I immediately felt myself relax. I was home.

Don W. sat at the head of a long table, tapped his lighter on the edge, took the cigar from his mouth, and called the meeting to order. "This is Quad A," he said, "AA for atheists and agnostics and anyone else with a desire to stop drinking." He was a small man with a gray goatee who spoke in an easy, soft voice. "We're here to talk about alcoholism so let me start by telling you what it was like for me," and he launched into his lead.

He explained that some people believe in God as a higher power or a power greater than themselves and that helped them stay sober. He said we didn't have to do that. All we had to do was to recognize and acknowledge a power – any power – greater than ourselves. He said many people use the group or AA itself as their higher power.

"That's cool," I thought. "The group works for me."

Don finished up by saying that God had nothing to do with his being a drunk and God had nothing to do with sobering up because he never met a god small enough to fit inside his head. He said it was us, the good people around the tables, who kept him sober and that we are why he kept coming back, because it was the only way he knew to deal with his disease.

Don's message was calm, positive, and reassuring but when he opened the meeting to comments, it became clear that not everyone possessed his serenity. Some people expressed outrage, others confusion, and a number said they weren't grateful to be alcoholics.

Paul V., a white-haired, cantankerous sailor, complained about the intolerance of the religious hypocrites in the program. Kansas City Len denounced the step Nazis as brainless brutes. Eva M. told us she wasn't sure if she was an alcoholic and was just following court orders. Larry W., the bemused newsman, revealed how he'd kept a pint in his desk at the paper to help him write but that his writing had seemed to improve since he dumped the bottle and began to attend meetings. John T., a querulous lawyer, argued Bill W. couldn't have it both ways – either alcoholism was a disease or the result of character flaws, but not both. And Railroad Bill angrily noted that the only two things he was ever entirely ready for was to have sex and eat a good meal.

These were my people. Most were Boomers gone bad, 60s radicals overwhelmed by their addictions, but still disrespectful, defiant, verbal, and outraged. Most admitted to being dually addicted, many reported DUIs, and a few, like me, had spent some time in jail.

But there was energy in the room, a determination to stand and fight, not let alcohol and drugs overwhelm us, and Don's calm cool at the head of the table assured us it was possible. He had been sober for years and had started this meeting in 1975, "so I could get together and not pray with a bunch of drunks like myself". He reassured me that I could be a sober atheist and I kept coming back.

Week by week, Don told us many things. He agreed AA wasn't a perfect program or organization but all we had to do was take what worked for us and leave the rest. He said the program was simple: don't drink and go to meetings. He said working the steps was probably a good idea and so was going to ninety meetings in ninety days. He said having a sponsor helped many people but if you weren't so inclined, that wasn't necessary. "Don't pick up that first drink," he said, "go to a meeting, and you'll be fine".

When people got excited about God, denouncing him and his cohorts, his priests, and the congregations that gathered on Sundays to sing hymns and pass the collection plate, Don advised them not to get worked up. "We don't need God to stay sober. We have each other."

At that time Don's Monday night Quad A meeting was the only meeting for atheists and agnostics in Chicago and I knew I needed more than one meeting a week to stay sober. I'd been a daily drinker and although I didn't do ninety in ninety, during my first six months in the program, I usually made six meetings a week.

The Quad A group kept me grounded and when people claimed you had to get on your knees first thing in the morning and last think at night or you'd be drunk again, I knew that wasn't true. I didn't have to pray. I had to attend meetings.

Sometimes I heard nonsense but I also heard a lot of good advice from both atheists and religious people about how to handle stress, anger, and the ups and downs of daily life, how to get along with others (a skill I always been too drunk to refine and develop) and how to live as a responsible, reasonable adult who didn't need a drink to get through the day (or night).

When I told some people I was an atheist, they assured me I'd drink again unless I changed my ways and got with God. They were wrong. I knew that. Don had told me they were wrong and what he told me was true. I haven't drunk again.

Don also had a great way to end our meetings. He'd say, "That's it for tonight, so we'll end in our usual way without saying anyone's prayer". There were nods and chuckles and people would drift off into the night with satisfied smiles on their faces.

We still end the Monday night Quad A meeting that way but we're no longer alone. There are currently a dozen atheist/agnostic meetings in the city and suburbs, each one doing things its own way but still implementing Don's basic philosophy: "Take what you need and leave the rest".

That's a flexible, effective approach to the program. It's worked for me, kept me sober, and that's why I keep coming back.

30. Life on Life's Terms

Frank M.

I stood there on my front lawn in handcuffs, to this day I'm not sure why. I had swallowed about a hundred Vicodin and an equal amount of Valium. It hadn't fully hit me yet, but I was definitely feeling pretty mellow. I didn't want a fight. I just wanted out.

A noisy argument with my wife had precipitated this little episode. Although I hadn't threatened her physically, I'd frightened her enough to prompt a call to 911. There would be a domestic disturbance incident on my record now. I was furious. That was the final humiliation for me. Time to check out.

My poor, long suffering wife, who had stood by me for many years through all my drinking and drugging and infidelities, watched me from the porch. I looked back up at her from the street, knowing that I might not ever see her again. I chose my final words carefully.

"You bitch, you killed me," I said.

And I felt well justified in that. This wasn't my fault, you see. It never was. But someone had to take the blame. She happened to be handy.

So then, let me back up a bit now and explain how I got there.

Not all alcoholics grew up in alcoholic homes, but I did. I didn't know anything was wrong with my world. I had nothing to compare it to. I just assumed that all mothers sat down on the end of their kids' beds at two in the morning with fragrant, clinking glasses of bourbon in their hands, and spent the wee hours till dawn telling stories with no endings, while alternately laughing and weeping. Turned out... not that many.

My adoptive mother was a mean and violent drunk who suffered from paranoid delusions. When I was three, she became convinced that my five year old sister and I were conspiring to kill her. That's ridiculous, of course. It wasn't until I was at least twelve years old or more that I began to really wish she were dead. I withstood three more years of daily physical and verbal abuse before I left home at fifteen.

Whether I was naturally inclined to being fearful or whether it was entirely a learned response is a question I'll likely never have an answer to. Either way, I eventually developed generalized anxiety disorder, which is a fancy way of saying that just about everything scared the hell out of me.

That is, until I found alcohol and pills.

The first time I got drunk (and high, though I never really got into weed) I looked over at my best buddy Jim and I said something like, "You gotta get here man... to where I am. It's wonderful."

And it was. I was free from fear and anxiety. I could breathe easy and let my shoulders fall down from my ears. I liked it. I liked it a whole lot.

It wasn't until I reached my mid-thirties that it stopped working. Not all at once – there were still bright moments. But steadily and progressively the lows were getting lower, and the highs were getting lower. The downpour of near constant anxiety had provided a fertile ground for depression to grow and flourish. I tried to treat that the same way I'd been treating my anxiety, with more drinking and drugging. It didn't work.

Then came the arrest for cocaine possession. My life's journey was supposed to lead to fame and fortune. That was the plan, anyway. Sitting in a jail cell across from another man defecating and asking if I had any paper he could wipe with? That was something of an unscheduled stop for me. And a wake-up call.

I started attending AA meetings, even though I didn't see my drinking as the biggest problem at that point. They were every-where, and honestly I didn't see what difference it made which Anonymous meeting I attended. Addiction was addiction in my mind. I raised my hand as a newcomer and found a sponsor at my first meeting. He asked me to read some things in the manual they called the Big Book. I did. I saw that I did in fact fit a certain pattern that was typical of alcoholics. As for the Steps themselves, I had no clear idea what they were supposed to be about. The God as you understood Him thing I comprehended even less. I just took it for granted that this stuff worked. Why else would it have been around for all these years?

I did an inventory. My sponsor and I read it together. We talked about how I had been selfish, and self-centered, dishonest and irresponsible. (I didn't note at the time how all this didn't jibe well with the "alcoholism is an illness" talk I'd been hearing.) He sent me home with instructions to sit silently for an hour, and then to follow the directions in the Big Book for Steps Six and Seven. I did.

Nothing much happened. And I still had no clear idea what the God thing was supposed to be about.

I kept going to meetings. I wrote my Eighth Step list, and began making my Ninth Step amends. I was staying sober, but now I was constantly filled with the anxiety that I'd been self-medicating all my life. And the black dog of depression was turning up at my door more and more regularly.

My first sponsor relapsed. My new sponsor picked up where I'd left off with the steps. He got me writing Tenth Step inventories on pretty much a nightly basis. I never noticed that they helped much. I did, however, identify a whole host of new character defects. Grandiosity, low self-esteem, unreasonable expectations, envy, sloth, anger and all the other deadly sins, plus many, many more insidious faults and flaws. Mainly this just served to make me feel a lot worse about myself. I wasn't directed to any effective tools for correcting these things.

I prayed the Seventh Step prayer most every night, asking a God I didn't understand or believe in to help make me a better person. I said the Third Step prayer at least a dozen times a day. Meanwhile my depression was starting to generate suicidal ideations. I began to dwell more and more on how much I needed some kind of mental relief.

Flash forward a year and I was again downtown buying cocaine. That began several cycles of staying sober for a year, or two, or even four once, and then succumbing to the desperate need for release from the psychic pain. Often the relapse occurred soon after I realized I'd been taking more than the usual notice of high seaside cliffs with sharp curves and long straightaways leading up to them.

It all culminated with the intentional overdose and the tawdry lawn show for my neighbors. I'd been taking antidepressants at that time, but they were no longer effective. I was involuntarily consigned to a lockdown psychiatric ward. While there, I volunteered to try electroshock therapy. After eight rounds, most of the previous two years of my life had been erased from memory. But the darkness of suicidal depression lifted. I was free to go.

Four months later the anxiety and depression returned. Soon after that, my wife found me drinking vodka in the garage out of a bottle I kept hidden in an old piece of luggage.

I returned once again to AA. There I was told that my relapses were the result of not doing the work, or not doing it correctly. "If your program isn't working, why don't you try ours?" my sponsor told me. I suspected it might be a little more complicated than that. I'd been involved in some biotech research years before, and I knew that blaming the patient for the failure of the therapy (or even for a high dropout rate) was unacceptable.

So what was going on here? Why wasn't this working for me?

I dove into researching AA history, hoping to get a better understanding of what this thing was supposed to be about. And what I found fairly shocked me. Faith-healing. Classical AA theory, such as it is, described what happened in AA under the operation of the Twelve Steps as a kind of facilitated faith-healing. I learned that when the Big Book talked about miracles, the language there wasn't metaphorical. Being probably beyond human aid, you need God the Father to work a full on miracle for you. And then you have to follow His direction, or His miraculous protection goes away. Begin with your best understanding of Him, and you will find Him eventually.

That was traditional AA's message.

I had little doubt that supernatural miracles and telepathic guidance from the Creator of the universe were not the actual operative factors in twelve step recovery. Contempt prior to investigation? Not really. For years I had prayed for miracles and guidance. It wasn't working.

So if outright supernatural miracles weren't getting the job done here in AA, what was? That's what I set out to learn.

What I found was us. Fallible humans struggling to stay mindful of our alcoholic conditions. Supporting and inspiring each other.

Working together to build lives we didn't have to run from into a bottle, or to puff up with artificial highs.

We're all crazy, someone told me once, but we're not all crazy at the same time. I began my new recovery by borrowing the judgment of my saner fellows, particularly when it came to the question of whether or not to take that first drink. Then I set myself on a course to become someone who didn't *need* to drink anymore. I found particularly good advice on that matter in certain Stoic philosophers and Buddhist ideas.

I learned about how to live life on life's terms, something I now believe to be the central mechanism behind many if not most recoveries. It's always changing, but here's my current understanding of what those terms are:

As an alcoholic, life is not offering me the option to drink moderately. As a human, life will not grant me any reliable picture of the future, nor any permanence, nor any control over much but my own choices.

I will learn only by testing my limits and my ideas in the real world, and some failure will be certain and at times painful. I will not be able to change the things I'm having difficult feelings about by manipulating those feelings. Not with chemicals, or sex, or any other form of evasion or manipulation.

I will be separated from the things and people I love by distance and by death. And I will be forced to spend precious minutes in the company of fools, and one of them will at times be me.

But I will be able to appreciate and even to create some beauty. I will be allowed to love, and to forgive. I will be awed by you and what you can show me that I couldn't see through my own eyes.

I will have my triumphs, and together we will revel in them. I will have my losses and you will console me.

And I will laugh in appreciation of our stumbling humanity, our courage, our insane hope in the face of everything that's stacked against us.

Life on life's terms. All in all, it's a fair offer.

In AA meetings, the speakers often end their stories with a description of "what it's like now." I'd like to do the same. My wife and I are about to celebrate another anniversary. We're honestly happy together. The business we own continues to support us well.

I began and finished writing two novels in the last fourteen months. I take great satisfaction in that, because I had never been able to keep myself at any project more than a few weeks while I was getting loaded.

I sought out and found my birth mother. She had been looking for me too over many years, as it turns out. She's a woman of depth and determination and in possession of a huge heart. I love her very much.

Life isn't always sunny now. But whatever it is, I'm there to greet it each day as some version of my better self. That's all I ever really needed or wanted to do. The wisdom of others and the strength of the AA community made it possible.

AA Agnostica

AA Agnostica is a website (aaagnostica.org).

AA Agnostica is a publisher.

AA Agnostica is a space for AA agnostics, atheists and freethinkers worldwide.

In all of those roles, AA Agnostica attempts to be a helping hand for the alcoholic who reaches out to Alcoholics Anonymous for help and finds that she or he is disturbed by the religious content of many AA meetings.

AA Agnostica is not affiliated with any group in AA or any other organization. Contributors to the AA Agnostica website – or to our books – are all members of Alcoholics Anonymous, unless otherwise indicated. The views they express are neither their groups' nor those of AA, but solely their own.

There is an increasing number of groups within AA that are not religious in their thinking or practice. These groups don't recite prayers at the beginning or ending of their meetings, nor do they suggest that a belief in God is required to get sober or to maintain sobriety. If the readings at their meetings include AA's suggested program of recovery, then a secular or humanist version of the 12 Steps is shared.

If you asked members of AA who belong to these nonreligious groups about their vision of the fellowship, they would probably describe it this way:

> *Alcoholics Anonymous is a fellowship of men and women who share their experience, strength and hope with each other that they may solve their common problem and help others recover from alcoholism. The only requirement for AA membership is a desire to stop drinking. There are no dues or fees for membership: we are self-supporting through our own contributions. AA is not allied with any sect, denomination, politics, organization or institution: neither endorses nor opposes any causes. Our primary purpose is to stay sober and help other alcoholics to achieve sobriety.*

AA Agnostica does not endorse or oppose any form of religion or atheism. Our only wish is to ensure suffering alcoholics that they can find sobriety in AA without having to accept anyone else's beliefs or having to deny their own.

The word "Agnostica" is derived from Chapter Four of *Alcoholics Anonymous*, otherwise known as the "Big Book". When we use the word "agnostic" in relation to AA – or words like "atheist" or "free-thinker" – we are simply referring to the specific wisdom of groups and individuals within the fellowship who understand that a belief in "God" is not necessary for recovery from alcoholism. It is the experience, strength and hope of these women and men which form the basis for the pages and posts on the AA Agnostica website and its published works and which are meant to be a comfort and an inspiration for others in AA.

Made in the USA
Columbia, SC
09 April 2018